A History of
APPLEDORE

Sir John Winnifrith

Phillimore

First published 1973
Second edition 1983

Published by
PHILLIMORE & CO. LTD.
Shopwyke Hall, Chichester, Sussex

ISBN 0 85033 485 3

Printed and bound in Great Britain by
BILLING & SONS LIMITED

CONTENTS

LIST OF PLATES
(between pages 26 and 27)

Abbreviations
A.C. = Archaeologia Cantiana
A.S.C. = Anglo-Saxon Chronicle
D.N.B. = Dictionary of National Biography
P.C.C. = Principal Probate Court of Canterbury

PREFACE

This account of Appledore is dedicated to the memory of Dr. William Cock, J.P., M.D., M.S., F.S.A., and to the people of Appledore. A dedication of Dr. Cock's memory is the least tribute I can offer, because, almost certainly, I would never have attempted this task without the material collected by him.

The Cocks had long been established in different parishes of Romney Marsh when, in 1828, William Cock, Dr. Cock's grandfather, became the tenant of Court Lodge and Court Lodge Farm. Dr. Cock himself was born in London in 1858, where his father, Dr. Frederick Cock, practised as an anaesthetist and physician. He himself succeeded to the combined practice but spent all the time he could on the Marsh. When he retired he came to live at Well House, Appledore, and was able to indulge his lifelong interest in antiquarian research. He had become a member of the Kent Archaeological Society in 1898, and during his lifetime he contributed seven articles to *Archaeologia Cantiana*. In 1902 he was elected a Fellow of the Society of Antiquaries.

When he died aged 85, in 1943, his granddaughter, Miss Rosina Cock, gave his manuscript books and papers to Miss Dorothy Johnston of Hallhouse Farm, Appledore, and she in turn left them to the care of the tenant for the time being of her house. In this capacity I have had access to them.

Dr. Cock undoubtly intended to write a history of Appledore and his note books and other papers were intended to provide the material for this. Some of them go back to 1899. At times he included his own reflections in medieval Latin. One, translated, reads, "God grant that I may live to finish this work". It was not to be. He got so interested in the hunt for more material - a task in which was helped by his friends Arthur Hussey and A. H. Taylor, the Tenterden antiquary - that no time was left for the final process of distilling a narrative from the great reservoir he had filled in the course of half a century of work. I only hope that I have done justice to his diligence. Clearly I have had to select, and in the process omit, much of the material he had amassed.

In general Dr. Cock concentrated on purely local records. If I have added anything, it has come from research into printed and other records from national and other collections which touch on Appledore.

With the example before me of Dr. Cock unable to consummate the labours of a lifetime, I have probably erred in taking too little time to

v

check the accuracy of my narrative and to fill in some of the gaps that remain. The most obvious omission is the account of the events of the last hundred years. Material for this is being collected but it will be more suitable, I think, for such recent events to be recorded publicly by a later generation. I shall be very glad to be told of any omissions and of any inaccuracies in what I have written.

It remains to thank all of those who have helped me in this work. I am grateful to Mr. Patric Dickinson for research in the Public Record Office, to Dr. Roger Prior for a note on the Lydd records, and to my son Dr. Thomas Winnifrith for getting me material in a number of specialist books which I needed to consult. Dr. Felix Hull, the County Archivist, enabled me to find a number of records in Maidstone, and Miss A. Oakley, the archivist of Canterbury Cathedral, was most kind in helping me to get material from the transcripts of the parish registers and from the remaining records of the Manor of Appledore. Miss Anne Roper has given me much good and greatly needed advice. Mr. Gordon Bourne very kindly gave me access to the records of Appledore allotments. The Vicar of Appledore, the Rev. A. Towse, allowed me to make a prolonged study of the books kept by the Overseers of the Poor. Mrs Mary Want of Ashford produced the sketch maps of the Rother seaways and of the Street.

Finally I cannot thank suffiently my wife for typing the first draft of the narrative, and Mrs. Gordon Bourne for making the fair draft.

The above, subject to a few corrections was written by me in 1973 when I published the first edition of this history. It has been out of print for some years and Messrs Phillimore are now publishing this new edition. This has enabled me to correct some errors, to rearrange and rewrite some passages and to add five further plates and three new appendices. There is also now an index. I record my thanks to Mrs. Gordon Bourne for typing the new material.

I am most grateful to Paddy Aiken A.R.P.S. for all the trouble she took to produce the charming front cover and Plates 2,3,5 and 13.

JOHN WINNIFRITH

Appledore, 1983

1

THE ROMAN OCCUPATION

When the Romans first occupied this part of Kent, the land and the sea coast looked vastly different. If you believe Nennius, who wrote in the ninth century, there was once an archipelago of 340 islands where Romney Marsh now stands. The islands were surrounded by 340 rocks, each with an eagle's nest on it, and into the rock girt sea flowed 340 rivers to form a single estuary called the Limen. You can perhaps discount his addiction for 340 of everything and substitute herons for eagles, but his general impression of what the Marsh once looked like is probably not far wrong. The Marsh, when the Romans first explored this part of Kent, was a great delta of sea creeks through which the tide flowed far inland, and into which the Limen, now the Rother, discharged its waters. Within the delta a considerable amount of land was already above sea level, but the whole area was cut up by a network of dykes or fleets into which the tide made its way, and a great deal of the lowland was permanently under water. There cannot be any certainty about where the main waterways ran or when Romney Marsh proper was first won from the sea by the building of the Rhee Wall. It is clear that an arm of the sea extended as far as the cliffs below Lympne where the Romans built the port, and later, the fortress of Portus Lemanis. The lie of the land makes it possible for the tide to have made its way towards Appledore along a creek following the line of the present Royal Military Canal, and at some period there was clearly an inlet up the low ground below Kenardington Church. Whether the Rother at this period ran into the sea along this channel is more doubtful. It is physically possible and it is plausible to suggest that Port Lemanis was the port on the estuary of the Limen.

What is certain is that, early in the Christian era, or just before it, the Rhee wall was built. Since its purpose was to keep the sea from flooding the marsh to the east, it is reasonable to assume that there was at that time, as there was certainly later, a sea channel flowing from the sea near Greatstone to Appledore and beyond it, through the low land between it and the hills above Reading Street, to Smallhythe. With this outlet available, most land water from this area would have made its way to the sea along this channel rather than through the fast silting water way to Lympne.

Who built the Rhee Wall and when is not known. It is claimed confidently that it was built, before the Roman invasion, by the

1

Belgic inhabitants who had crossed the Channel from the Low Countries, bringing with them the art of embankment, which has indeed left its mark in the great earthworks, the Terpen, of Friesland. Others think that the Romans set the conquered Britons to work on this immense task so as to increase the land area near their settlement at Lympne. Either theory may be right. There is no archaeological proof, and the first documentary evidence of the Rhee Wall comes well after the Norman invasion. The best argument for its early construction is that the Saxons were most unlikely to have built it. Rhee is also, probably, a Celtic word for river.

Of more significance to Appledore in this period was the condition of the low land between it and the cliffs from St. Michael's Tenterden to Reading Street, Smallhythe and beyond. There is considerable evidence that, at this time and for many centuries later, the Rother ran from Bodiam and Newenden past Ebony through the Rhee channel to meet the sea near Greatstone. It is also most probable that at this time all the low land round Ebony was permanently under water, so that Ebony was an island and shallow water separated Appledore from Stone.

Walland Marsh, all the land west of the Rhee wall, was still open to the sea, though Lydd and other parts near the coast were above the water level. The sea itself flowed all round Rye and up the Brede and Tillingham valleys, and a creek very likely extended from Rye as far as the point where the inland sea round Ebony drained into the Rhee Channel.

At this point in history, therefore, Appledore probably stood on a low promontory looking across a shallow inland sea to the high ground where Stone in Oxney stood, to the isle of Ebony, and to the hills above Reading Street. To the south they may well have had communications with Romney by the Rhee wall, but to the south-west Lydd was the only dry area in Walland Marsh which was probably as waterlogged as the area round Ebony.

Kent as a whole played a key part in the Roman conquest and occupation of this island during the first 500 years of the Christian era. The Kentish coast provided their first landing beaches. From the great Roman ports at Sandwich, Dover and Lympne, roads were built to provide rapid communications with London and thence, by the great network of roads fanning out from London, with the rest of the country. From Lympne, Stone Street provided a first-rate link, through Canterbury, with Watling Street. At a later stage, a road was driven, still traceable between Tenterden and Lympne, which provided lateral communications between the different roads from London and the ports of Kent and Sussex.

During the greater part of Roman rule, Appledore would have been little use to the Romans in developing their communication system. The Romans were established in settlements at Lympne and Dymchurch but the waterlogged state of the land to the north of

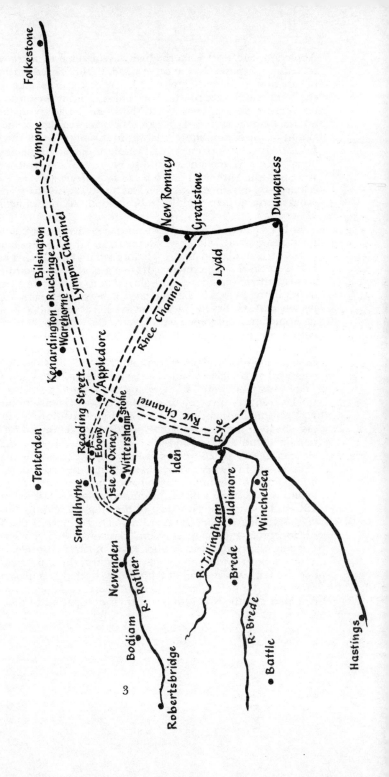

3

Appledore cut it off from the highways and a port there would have served no purpose. On the other hand, in the last century of Roman occupation, the situation changed. The Saxon tribes started to raid the Kent and Sussex coasts. Their ships could move up any convenient creek or seaway and the Romans had to organise a coastal defence system under an officer named significantly "The Count of the Saxon Shore". It was in this period that the Romans built their great fortresses at Dover, Lympne and Pevensey, of which such impressive remains are still to be seen. Possibly, it was at this time that the Mithras altar, to be seen in Stone church, was set up at Stone and, and since Mithraism was a cult most widely adopted in the Roman army, there could have been a military detachment posted in Oxney.

Other small military outposts in the Rother estuary would have been desirable, if only as watch posts, and if there was a military post at Stone, a similar post at Appledore would have been a useful link. However there is no evidence of such a post or indeed of any Roman settlement at Appledore. A single denarius, dug up in a garden of a house in the Street, is the sole tangible evidence of any Roman presence. A. G. Bradley, when he lived at Rye, paid a number of visits to Appledore, and joined with Doctor Cock, the historian of Appledore, in exploring the village. In *The Old Gate of England* he suggests that the knoll on the hill beyond Court Lodge, beyond which extends the level to Oxney, contains the "remains of a Roman camp". The trenches visible on the hill are definitely not Roman. They were made when soil was dug to fill the old dyke to Oxney in the last century. Bradley does not give any evidence in support of his proposition, and, until this is proved by excavation, his theory can only be hypothesis. Any Roman settlement at Appledore has so far remained undiscovered and the only safe conclusion is that in Roman times Appledore was of little significance. The single Roman coin dug up in the garden of Saxton House in 1905, though in itself no evidence of continuous occupation, is interesting. It is a silver denarius of Sabina, wife of the emperor Hadrian, issued in about 130 A.D. On its front is a bust of the empress with the inscription "Sabina Augusta Hadriani Aug.P.P.". On the back is the representation of Concordia and the inscription "Concordia Aug.". When dug up, the coin was coated with a thick layer of silver chloride, the result of a long deposit in the soil. In all probability, the soil in which it had been so long was the soil of Appledore. In that case Romans, even if they made no permanent settlement there, certainly came to Appledore in the first century of their occupation of this country.

4

2

SAXONS AND DANES
The Great Danish Invasion

The Jutes who now, in the sixth century, conquered and occupied
Kent and part of Hampshire, gave Appledore its first proven settlement. The invaders had little interest in the magnificent road system
of the Romans. Sea and river ways were much more to their liking,
and Appledore with its many creeks leading to the sea would have
struck them as a highly suitable place in which to found a settlement.
Although no trace has been found of any Jutish occupation, either of
buildings or of burials, there is no doubt that the Jutes lived here and
called the place Apuldre.*

The proof comes from a dramatic account in the Anglo Saxon
Chronicle, under the year 892, of the great Danish invasion in that
year which made its first landing at Apuldre. The text which follows
is taken from G. M. Garmonsway's translation in the Everyman's library
of the Parker M. S.

"892. In this year the great host about which we formerly
spoke went again from the east kingdom (Flanders) westward to
Boulogne, and were there provided with ships, so that they
crossed in one voyage, horses and all, and then came up into the
mouth of the Lympne with two hundred and fifty ships. That
estuary is in East Kent at the end of the great forest which we
call Andred (the Weald—then thickly wooded) . . . The river
flows out from the forest; they rowed their ships up as far as the
forest, four miles from the entrance to the estuary, and there
they stormed a fort within the fen; occupying it were a few
peasants and it was half built. Then soon after this Haesten came
with eighty ships into the mouth of the Thames, and made
himself a fort at Milton Royal and the other host at Appledore.

893. And then King Alfred gathered his levies and marched so
that he was encamped between the two hosts, and at a convenient distance from the stronghold in the forest and the
stronghold on the water, so that he could overtake either if they
wished to make for any open country. Then afterwards they
moved through the woods in gangs and bands, wherever the
margin was left unguarded; and almost every day other troops
both from the levies and also from the forts, went to attack
them (either by day) or by night . . . Only twice did the host

*For a discussion of the meaning of the name see Appendix I.

come out from the camps in full force; on the one occasion when they first landed, before the levies were mustered, and on the other occasion when they wished to evacuate their positions."

The chronicle of the year 893 goes on to describe how Haesten, the Danish leader, after collecting much plunder, decided to move into Essex, where he was wounded. A great battle took place at Benfleet, where Haesten had built a fort, to which he had moved "the host which had been encamped at Milton and in addition the great host had arrived there, which had been encamped at Appledore at the mouth of the Lympne". The Saxon army stormed the fort, while Haesten was out on a plundering expedition, seized the women and children, including Haesten's wife and his two sons, and brought them to London. Alfred restored them to Haesten. One of the boys was his godson.

With incredible energy, Haesten, with the rest of his forces, managed to fit in two more campaigns this year, one up the Thames to the Severn, and another to Chester. In 894 he was raiding in Wales. In 895 he was back on the Lea, before moving off again to the Severn. Only in 896 did he abandon his attempt to establish a permanent settlement in England. "By the mercy of God" the Chronicle says, "he had not utterly crushed the English people."

Haesten's invasion was far from being the first attempt by the Danes to seize and colonise England. The Chronicle records the first raid as taking place in 789, and Kent was an early target. "Many of the people of Romney Marsh" were slain in 841. Shortly, however, before King Alfred succeeded to the throne in 870, the pace quickened, and it was evident that the invaders came not to raid but to settle. King Alfred throughout his reign had to fight time and again to confine them to East Anglia, and, after his treaty with Guthrum at Wedmore in 878, he might have hoped that, though the Danes had secured a permanent footing in East Anglia and Northumbria, they were at any rate confined to this part of England, and in general living peaceably with their English neighbours. Haesten's invasion was a rude reminder that the appetite of the Danes was far from satisfied.

A number of points emerge from the text of the Chronicle which are of particular relevance to Appledore.

The invading fleet, the ship-borne army (the sciphere) which sailed up to Appledore, was an exceedingly large one. There is no reason to doubt the Chronicle's figure of 250 ships, holding horses as well as men, carrying an invasion force of perhaps 5,000 men. It must have been an army of these dimensions to have kept King Alfred fighting for five years before he could dislodge them. Clearly he had no doubt of the significance of the invasion based on Appledore.

For the local population, this vast fleet of longships rowing up the sea creek must have been a terrifying sight. Only fifty years had passed since the men of Romney Marsh had been slaughtered in large numbers by the Danes. They knew the appalling savagery they could expect once the Danes had landed. There can be little doubt what happened to the few peasants who were manning the half-built fort which the Danes stormed, before landing to build the earthwork which was to be their main base for the first part of the campaign.

Where this half-built fort was sited, and where the invading Danes under Haesten built their encampment, cannot be deduced with any certainty. The English half-built fort was "four miles from the entrance to the estuary". If we can be certain that this means four miles from where the estuary joined the sea, the problem still remains to define where this junction with the sea was in the greatly different situation of the sea and land in those days. The choice for Haesten's approach lay probably between the Rhee channel, which joined the sea between Old and New Romney, and the Appledore to Rye Channel, the mouth of which in those days was near modern Rye. (See the sketch map on page 3.) The half-built fort, under the first hypothesis, was within the fen, on the Rhee Wall, four miles from modern Appledore. Under the second, it could have been somewhere near where the Isle of Oxney falls away to join the fen near Knock. There is just as much doubt about the site of the encampment on which was based, first the whole invasion force, and later the whole force, less the detachment of 80 ships—about a third of their total strength—which sailed off to make an encampment at Milton Regis on the Swale near Sittingbourne. (This latter camp is identified either as Rough Castle at Milton, next to the great Bowater factory, or Bayford Castle on Milton Creek.) Clearly it was a large encampment to hold so large a force, and equally clearly, like the two camps at Milton, it must have been near enough to the seaway to protect the ships of the expedition from attack. Stone has been suggested, but a more likely site is the "island" of mediaeval and modern Appledore, which has the street for its spine, and then, as now, stands above the marshes surrounding it on both sides.

The many topographers who have written about Appledore have created the myth that Haesten and his Danes built a substantial stone castle like the remains of the Roman fortresses at Lympne and Pevensey, or the Norman castle at Hastings. The Danes, who were at Appledore for no more than a few months, had neither the time nor the skill to build stone fortresses. They were content to throw up earthworks—earth, revetted with turves, surrounded by a wall of pales. The Saxons made similar fortifications, and all these fortifications were referred to by the English peasants as "castles" as for instance at Castle Rough, already referred to, and Castle Toll at Newenden. The earthwork at Appledore was clearly a substantial affair, but if it was round Appledore village it needed little more work than some cutting to steepen the natural slope of the "island", and a palisade round the perimeter. (For the myth of Appledore Castle see Appendix II.)

7

Haesten's use of Appledore emerges from the Chronicle. It served him primarily as his first main base for his future campaign, which was to take him as far afield as London, the West Country, Wales and Cheshire. This base, however, was evacuated once he was ready to move on. The Chronicle makes it clear that "the great host which had been encamped at Appledore" which had already before then lost one-third of its strength when 80 ships were sent off to build the encampment at Milton, had left Appledore and had arrived at Benfleet in Essex, less than twelve months after their first landing there.

The Chronicle also throws light on the tactics of both Haesten and King Alfred. Immediately after arrival the whole Danish force moved out on a reconnaissance of the surrounding country. After that there was no further sally *en masse* till the time when they evacuated their position to move to Benfleet. In the intervening months Haesten was content to send out patrols (by night as well as by day) into the heavily wooded Weald. Simultaneously King Alfred made the basis of his tactics the construction of encampments between Appledore and Milton, from which his men almost every day went out to engage the Danish patrols. Almost certainly the earthwork at Castle Toll was built by King Alfred to control the passage of the Rother, which at that time flowed from Newenden to Smallhythe. The earthwork at Kenardington may also be King Alfred's work during this phase of the campaign. Some have identified it as the site of Haesten's encampment, but surely it would have been too far from the seaway to give protection to his fleet.

Haesten's campaign did not "utterly crush the English people", and, presumably, it did not utterly destroy all the Jutish families living in and around Appledore. However, the people of Appledore, and indeed of all the surrounding villages, must have suffered terribly. Haesten's great army lived off the country, and the standard practice of the Danes, when foraging, was to slaughter, plunder, and burn. All the cattle, apart from any driven off in time to the forests, would have been slaughtered, the hay would have been taken for the Danish horses, the corn for the army. The choice for any of the people who survived, was either starvation or a long flight into the Weald to find the protection of King Alfred's ffyrd, the Home Guard of the day.

It is not known when Appledore was resettled. The Danish forays into England were by no means over. They continued intermittently right into the eleventh century. Kent was not, however, so often a target. Olaf Tryggvason raided Folkestone and its neighbourhood in 991, and Thurkil attacked Canterbury in 1009, but Appledore may not have been affected. What is known is that the village had again been settled under the protection of the church. A charter of 968, dealing with a complicated land transaction, mentions among the many parties who assented to it "the brotherhood of Apuldre". A charter of 1032 (when Canute was King), records that the manor of

Apuldre was conveyed to the convent of Christ Church Canterbury. The manor had therefore been in existence before that.

The peasants probably benefited by having the church rather than a layman as their landlord. The account of the Manor in Domesday Book records that 37 villeins and 41 borderers were working to provide part of the food for the monks of Canterbury. This suggests that the total population was some 300, quite a large community.

Another document—the Domesday Monachorum—lists the churches existing in this area of Kent at the time of the Norman invasion. Appledore church is amongst them, and almost certainly this pre-Norman church had been built by the Canterbury monks, who owned the manor and, with it, the advowson, the right to appoint the priest.

Appledore had therefore made a good recovery and was firmly established under the tutelage of the monks of Canterbury when England started to adjust itself to the rule of the Norman Kings. It seems to have been little affected by the battle of Hastings and the campaign which followed it. (See Appendix III for a discussion of the site of Harold's muster point and William's punitive raid on Romney.) There was little change in the life of the village.

3

Life under the Manor — The great storm of 1286 — A market granted
The arrival of the Horne family - The French burn Appledore - Wat Tyler's rising

The Archbishop and the monks of Canterbury had owned the manor of Appledore, and had in all probability been the patrons of its church, for some thirty years before the Norman invasion. What happened as a result of the change of régime is not too clear. The Domesday Monachorum describes the manor as belonging to the monks alone and leased by them at farm to one Robert of Romney. The Domesday Survey in 1086 states that the Archbishop (Lanfranc) had the manor back in demesne but a mutilated entry in a list (made in about 1170) of the Archbishop's tenants holding land by knight service suggests that Lanfranc may have let the manor out to farm again to a man with the unpromising name of Robert Fitz Wazo. If this is the right deduction, Appledore had again to submit to the exactions of a lord of the manor who set out to secure from them not only the sum required by the Archbishop but as much more as he could secure for himself. How long this system of farming out the manor went on is not certain. By the time Geoffrey held office as Prior of Canterbury (1191-1213) the manor was back again in the hands of the monks.

Whatever the effect of having a layman "farming" the manor in these earlier years, Appledore was by then a reasonably flourishing community.

The Rhee channel to Romney and the channel to Rye were probably much as they had been when Haesten landed at Appledore. Ships could carry goods to and from Appledore, and this brought it prosperity. Its wealth is recorded in the Domesday Monachorum. It records the dues payable by certain churches before the appointment of Lanfranc in 1066. Appledore's annual quota was 7/- compared with, for example, 2/8d. from Lyminge, 9/8d. from Maidstone and 50/- from Folkestone. Appledore also paid one sester of honey, 30 loaves, 4 lambs, 7d. for oil and 6d. for wine. Domesday book itself, compiled in 1086 records that in that year there was a church and a fishery worth 3/4d. And the 37 villeins and 41 borderers had between them 11 ploughs.

Appledore at this time, with its population of some three hundred, was evidently, thanks to its position on the seaway, reasonably prosperous.

The monks of Canterbury had built Appledore's first church in Saxon times. The Domesday Monachorum records it as in existence before 1066. It can reasonably be assumed that the Canterbury monks were the patrons who built it and appointed the priest. No trace of this early church remains and we do not know to which saint it was dedicated. Archbishop Stephen Langton, consecrated in 1207, but kept out of England by King John till 1213, at some time before his death in 1228 gave the patronage of the church to the Prior and Monks of St. Martin's, Dover. The manor itself was retained for Canterbury. A manor record of 1248 shows Dover Priory as then owning land in Appledore, as do other documents of this period. The Dover monks were, therefore, not only patrons of the church but landowners in the parish. The architecture of the central portion of the church, the surviving hood moulding round the inside of the East window, the arches (both in the chancel and the nave) and the tower, show that it was built in the early thirteenth century and, quite possibly, the monks of Dover built it soon after they were given the patronage by Stephen Langton. A manor document of 1261 records an obligation to pay a quit rent in the churchyard of St Peter and St Paul, which must, almost certainly, refer to this Early English church. This seems to be the earliest record of its dedication. By the early thirteenth century there was certainly a stone church at Appledore in the Early English style, and it is this church which remains as the central core of the present building.

It has been maintained that the north chapel was built at an earlier stage. The main argument for this is that the two small lancet windows in its sanctuary and the sanctuary arch belong to an earlier style, and that the dark red sandstone used freely in the walls, and particularly in the quoins, is found only rarely in the rest of the church. The fragments of the Early English arch in the west wall of this chapel certainly raise doubt about its original extent, and the theory of a much smaller, rather earlier, church cannot be dismissed.

The church and the manor completely dominated the whole life of the village throughout most of this period. There never was a manor house nor a resident squire. The Lords of the Manor were represented in the village by their bailiff who sometimes, but not always, lived in the Court Lodge. The grip of the manor on the village was, however, total. The manor owned the whole of the land. All who lived in the village occupied their land, their houses and their shops, on the terms laid down by the manor. Fortunately a number of the manor records of this period have survived, and from them some inkling can be gained of the conditions in which the people lived.

The monks were far sighted landlords. They saw that the seaways, though a great asset, needed to be controlled. There is evidence, even in the earliest manor documents, of innings (inclausa) which they had carried out to produce water meadows where before there had been only saltings covered by the sea at high tide. Conditions in the leases of land to tenants of the manor were also carefully laid down to ensure that the tenants kept out both salt and fresh water from their holdings.

In a sense, too, all the tenants were "protected" tenants. Though they did not own their land and had to submit to the rents and other conditions laid down by the manor, they could not be turned off their holdings; nor could their descendants who inherited the right of occupation from generation to generation. An early document, between 1191 and 1213, records a holding to be held by gavelkind, and the system probably applied throughout the manor. Gavelkind, the complicated land tenure of Kent, had many rules, the best known of which is the requirement that, on the death of a tenant, his land should pass not to his eldest son but to all his sons in equal portions. In theory all gavelkind tenants were free to sell or assign their land, subject to the consent of the manor. In practice this consent was granted much more freely to "free" tenants than to the serfs. At the time of Domesday there were 78 serfs on the manor. Serfdom remained a practice in Kent up to the first part of the fifteenth century, and the church manors were not immune from this barbarous system. There is no reason to think that the manor of Appledore did not have serfs amongst its tenants for most, if not all, of the period covered in this chapter. Their main disability was that consent was not, in practice, given to them to leave their holdings. Successive generations of tenants, if not technically serfs, were bound to their holdings with no choice but to submit to the rents and other conditions laid down by the manor. Of these the most burdensome was to provide service to the manor—so many days a year to be worked without payment, tilling and harvesting the demesne land of the manor.

The surviving documents record a number of cases where consent to sell or assign land was given by the manor. These provide information about the names of the tenants, the size of their holdings, and the names of the manor officials. Not surprisingly there are no records of refusal to agree to such transactions by disgruntled serfs on the manor.

Some of these twelfth- and thirteenth-century documents are grants by the manor to a tenant of a new holding, others the sale or leasing of a holding made by a tenant with the consent of the manor. Another category, no doubt encouraged by the vicar of the day, is the free gift of a holding handed over by the tenant to the monks of Canterbury, as an act of piety. Most of the tenants in all these cases are men who are referred to by their Christian names and the name of their holding, for example, John and Henry de Blakeburn and Henry de Goseburn, who in the thirteenth century are already on the way to giving their descendants the surnames of Blackburn and Gosborne. Others are referred to by their trade names, Geoffrey the Miller, Roger the Fisher, and so on. One twelfth-century grant is pretty clearly made to much humbler tenants. They are referred to simply as Robert, Simon, Richard and Adam. They are given holdings in gavelkind of some 10 acres apiece in the water meadow, for which they have to pay an annual rent of 14d. an acre. Names of the manor officials appear—William de Ginelsforde, Steward of the Manor in 1251, William de Haite, Bailiff of the Manor in 1270, Gerard the Chaplain in 1257. Christian names show the gradual progression from Saxon to English—Hereward, Godebold and Ealwyn surviving, though many more were christened John, William and Thomas.

Many field names are given, unfortunately with little directions by which they can be identified:

    Cruckehame
    Cruchefeld
    le Staple
    Wellfield
    Porchfield
    Turrestune
    Tutulingehill, on the road leading to the bridge of Oxenea.
    Totelynghel (probably the same place) in the Dene called
      Blakeburn.
    Hothfeld
    Malmarsh
    Blakeburn beyond the wall of Staple.
    Catingehelde or Ketingheld (in the new inning)
    Threhornehamme
    Langenhamme
    Pendfield
    Dyersland
    Springebroke
    Estlode
    Anderkyngstreet
    Swalewe
    Kynehel next to wall Raipe (the Rhee Wall).

There is also a reference in a grant of 1191-1213 to "the green road through the middle of our marsh leading to the chapel of Fairfield". This probably followed much the same line as the present road. Unfortunately, in most cases, the descriptions are quite inadequate to identify the location of the holding.

This information from the manor rolls gives all too little material from which to assess the lot of the people of Appledore in those times. Under the monks of Canterbury, the manor at least spared them some of the worst privations of those times. The general prosperity of the parish gave some benefit to the poorer inhabitants, but their life was hard. The unpaid service they had to give on the manor demesne left them little enough time to earn wages or to manage their own smallholdings. The rents they paid for these were heavy; 14d. an acre was common. In the great rising of 1381 one of the demands was for a maximum rent of 4d. Life could not have been easy for most of the tenants on the manor at Appledore.

Three events towards the end of the fourteenth century were to be of considerable significance to the parish.

The first involved a gradual blocking of the main seaway - the Rhee channel, along which the Rother made its way to the sea from Bodiam to Newenden, Smallhythe, Reading Street and Appledore to Romney. (See map on page 5.) This channel was much more important to Romney than to Appledore, and for this reason the bed of the channel was vested in the jurisdiction of Romney all the way to Reading Street. It could be kept open only by the scouring of the ebb tide supplemented by the fresh water of the Rother. Already, in 1258, Henry III found it necessary to order a sluice to be made at Appledore to impound the seawater which flowed up Appledore's other channel, the creek to Rye harbour, so that this could be released down the Rhee channel and keep it scoured. In 1286, however, a great storm swept the shingle over the mouth of the channel at Romney and closed it to navigation, but, as a document of 1338 shows, a new channel was formed—when, precisely, is not certain—which up to 1349 kept navigation open to Appledore, and thence as far as Newenden.

Its reprieve did not last long. It seems likely that the great storm of 1286 had increased the eastward drift of the shingle and reduced the scouring of the Rother down the Rhee channel. The result was the final drying up of the Rhee channel. The course of the old channel can still be seen from the Appledore to Romney road, about thirty or forty yards from it on the seaward side.

The loss of this channel was far more disastrous to Romney than to Appledore. There was still the sea creek to Rye harbour. Appledore could trade with Rye and Winchelsea, and the tide could still carry ships up as far as Smallhythe and beyond.

A second significant event was the grant by Edward III to the Prior and monks of Christ Church, Canterbury, of the right to hold a weekly market in their manor of Appledore, and a yearly fair on the 11th of January. This right was given in 1359, and formally gave Appledore the status of a town, though in manor documents for many years before then the entries referred to it as a town (villa) and some of the inhabitants described themselves as of the "Tun". More important to the life of the parish was the trade resulting from the weekly market and the annual fair. This fair went on being held on its traditional site in the Street right to the end of the nineteenth century.

The third event in the fourteenth century was the arrival of the Horne family in the village. A Mathew de Horne and a John Horne were living in Winchelsea in 1277 and 1299, the latter in that year being pardoned for his part in the murder of a woman—"for good service"! Whether or not they were the progenitors of the Hornes of

Hornes Place, Appledore, the family were established there in 1366 when William de Horne was granted a licence by the Archbishop to hear mass in the lovely oratory of Hornes Place, which still survives and has been so admirably restored by the Ancient Monuments Department. A sketch of Hornes Place in 1857 and a photograph of the chapel are reproduced in Plates 1 and 2. Already William de Horne had, in 1359, been appointed a member of the corporation for maintaining Romney Marsh. Hornes Place was not a manor. It and the surrounding land were held of the manor of Appledore, and the Hornes paid a quit rent for it. However, without any doubt, the family had become prominent members of the county establishment, and were destined to have a considerable say in the affairs of the village.

Two episodes in national history struck Appledore in the last years of this century. Up to then, life on the manor seems to have gone on as in the past, and one entry in the records at least shows that justice could be secured. The manor court dealt not only with the land transactions of the manor, including the important business of collecting the rents; the Court Baron also handled a number of offences. In 1364 one John Clerk of Appledore petitioned the King to enquire into an assault on his house by more than eleven men from the village, who dragged out his wife and daughter and mistreated them and carried off his household goods and livestock. The King referred the petition to the Constable of Dover Castle. He promptly passed the buck to the Prior of Canterbury with many protestations that he did not wish to trespass on the jurisdiction of his manor. The Prior then replied that he had made enquiry, he had made all reasonable restitution, but in fact the incident was only a normal distraint. No doubt John Clerk hadn't paid his rent to the manor. John Clerk, his wife Juliana, and his daughter Joan had not got much in the way of amends, but at least the law of the land had come into operation.

This small local incident was soon to be overtaken by a major disaster to the village. England's sea power, which had secured complete mastery of the Channel in the early years of Edward III, had by now fallen into decay, and raids by the French on the south coast had become all too common. In 1377 and 1378 the Isle of Wight was captured, Winchelsea attacked and Rye and Hastings burned. In 1380 another series of French raids started. Appledore was one of the places burnt by the French. Most of the houses would have been built of wattle and daub. Most of the roofs would have been thatched. The firing of the town by the French probably meant the total destruction of all the houses in the street. The bare statement that Appledore was burned by the French comes from Holinshed but the firing of Appledore is confirmed by other sources, and there is no reason to doubt the statement.

In describing the raids of this year Thomas of Walsingham says how the French in a series of hit and run attacks "Villas, injectis

15

flammis, combusserunt" hurled in fire, and burnt the towns. Small cannon may have been used for in the previous year Walsingham mentions the use of machines "quod gunnas vocant". There is other physical evidence. The great archway into the tower from the church (there was no door from the churchyard into the belfry in those days) still bears the marks of fire as does the door of the bricked-up north porch. Finally, when the tiles were relaid in 1925, masses of charred embers were found, and it seems abundantly clear that the French fired the church with the rest of the village. There must have been great hardship for all the people left without shelter and with all their possessions destroyed.

Not surprisingly in the following year, when Wat Tyler's rising, the great Peasant's Revolt of 1381, took place, Appledore was involved. There were many reasons why the peasants came out. Serfdom and exactions by the manor was one of the main causes of dissent. In addition there was the great inequality of wealth between the gentry and the mass of the people. There the excessive wealth of the monks in the Regular Orders, like the Benedictines of Canterbury and Dover, and the poverty of the parish priests, a number of whom joined the rising. Finally there was the feeling that the young King Richard II was being kept in leading strings by his Ministers, whom the rebels regarded as traitors. These "traitors" were responsible for the misgovernment which led to high taxes to pay for futile expeditions against the French, and the disgrace of the French raids on the south coast resulting in the destruction of Rye, Winchelsea and Appledore. The last straw which set the rebellion in motion was the poll tax imposed on all including the poorest in the land, to pay for further hopeless attempts to win back the lost provinces in France.

The rising which resulted in bands of peasants marching on London from nearly all the villages in Kent and Essex, with simultaneous risings in Sussex, all the eastern counties, and in many other parts of England, was highly organised by the "magna societas"—the great confederacy. Orders were sent out to all parts of the country to do three things: to make local attacks on the traitors—the members of the establishment; to march on a number of muster points; and lastly to join in a concerted attack on London. Throughout their campaign, Wat Tyler's followers showed pathetic belief in the willingness of the boy King to right their wrongs. They carried the royal standard and their rallying cry was "King Richard and the Commons of Kent". They were loyal to him. All they wanted to do was to set him free. They were sure he would help their cause and restore good government.

In Appledore the local "traitor" was inevitably William Horne, already a member of the establishment and destined on July 20th, when the revolt had been suppressed and retribution was being exacted, to be appointed one of the Commissioners "pro resistendo

16

rebellibus et inimicis Regis"—for combating the rebels and the King's enemies.

Most of the local incidents, phase one in the plan of the "magna societas", are known only from the surviving legal records, the indictments eventually filed in the Kings Bench archives, and now known as the Ancient Indictments. One of these is a True Bill found against William of Apoldre, who "raised divers men at Apoldre and made insurrection against our Lord the King and his people on June 11th 1381, and compelled them to swear to accompany him, whose names are Gilbert of Wytresham (Wittersham), John Willeam and many others".

Meanwhile, the day before, two men in Cranbrook had raised a number of men in Tenterden and broke into the house of William de Horne at Apoldre, and carried off goods and chattels worth ten pounds. Another indictment, referring to what is probably the same incident, charges a number of men led by John Onewyne of Melkhouse (Sissinghurst) for knocking down "prostaverunt" the houses (*sic*) of William Horne at Appledore.

This incident followed a pattern common in Kent during the revolt, an attack on the house of a "traitor", seizure of property to finance the campaign and, usually, the destruction of the manorial records. Once these were destroyed, so the peasants thought, they would be free from the exactions of the manor. Whether the men of Appledore were involved in this incident at Hornes Place is not known. They may have concentrated on the records of the manor of Appledore. On July 10th, 1382, Sir Edward Dalyngrigge, who in 1386 was licensed to build Bodiam Castle, was given authority to "reconstitute" the manorial records of the Archbishop of Canterbury, destroyed by the rebels. Dalyngrigge was a close friend of Sir Henry Knollys, a veteran captain of the Hundred Years War, and the one man in London who had the will and capacity to turn the triumphs of the rebels into immediate defeat. In reconstituting the records Dalyngrigge would not have erred on the side of clemency to the tenants of the manor.

The legal records only occasionally give the verdict and the sentence "decollatus" or "suspensus" - beheaded or hanged and nothing is known of the fate of William of Appledore. In the ancient indictments a man called William Apuldre of Malling was charged with others for being one of the first disturbers of the peace. He also comes in the accounts of the escheator (the crown officer responsible for seizing any property of convicted felons) which shows that he was hanged and his property worth 2/- confiscated. He could be the same man. Rebels, in 1381, often used pseudonyms. The fact that he is called by his Christian name suggests that he was one of the poorer peasants. Surnames were by this time quite common in Appledore.

A man called Philip of Apoldre was also indicted for his part in a very strange conspiracy near Sissinghurst, which took place as late as

17

September 30th, long after the rebellion had been stamped out. Its quite hopeless object was to compel the King to restore the charters of liberty given to the rebels in the hour of success, and cancelled once the tide had turned against them. This plot is of great interest because it involved a plan to secure the throne for John of Gaunt. The leader of the conspiracy turned King's Evidence, was challenged to trial by combat by one of his fellow conspirators, who lost and was promptly drawn, hanged and quartered.

Clearly the men of Appledore took a leading part in the rebellion. Equally clearly retribution was heavy. With this and the village still recovering from the destruction caused by the French, this chapter of Appledore's history closes on a sombre note.

4

1381 TO THE EARLY TUDORS

Rebuilding after the French raid – Lollardry and Jack Cade's rising
The Hornes and the yeomen flourish – Life in the village centred on the church
The impact of the Reformation

If the experience of Rye and Winchelsea is a guide, the damage to the village caused by the French raids must have been appalling. The church was repaired and enlarged, and the work then done can be seen in the present building. None of the domestic buildings put up to replace those lost in the fire have survived. They were probably wattle and daub and, if any were timber framed, such timbers then used which remain today would have been incorporated in the more substantial houses built in the course of the sixteenth century. Hornes Place still retains the chapel, licensed in 1366, and some remnants of the original building, and it seems likely that the French contented themselves with destroying the houses in the Street and did not attack the Place.

Much work was done in the church. (Appendix II discusses the myth that the present church was built or rebuilt from the ruins of an ancient castle.) The extent of the fire can be traced to a certain extent by the evidence of the stones in the arch of the tower, and in the stone framework of the north door, bricked up since 1699. This stonework still shows the red marks left by the flames. Charred embers were also found on the floor of the nave in this area when the tiles were relaid in 1925. Another discovery at this time was the remains of a line of pillars extending from the north wall of the chancel. Finally an explanation has to be found for the curious alignment of the fourteenth-century roof built after the fire. Its ridge runs well off centre from the central line of the tower to the altar. A probable reconstruction of what happened is that the French fired the thatched roof of the Early English church. The timbers fell in, dragging with them the line of pillars which up to then had formed a north aisle. Faced with the problem of putting a new roof on the church, the woodwrights decided to build it higher, so as to span both the nave and what had been the north aisle. Inevitably this resulted in the somewhat lopsided alignment of the ridge beam and crown posts well to the north of the centre line of the chancel and nave. (See also Appendix VII.)

Much more remained to be done in the church. The screen separating the north and south chapels from the nave dates from this period, and must have been made soon after the fire. The central section is rather later. During this period also the south aisle and south chapel were reconstructed, though much of the work on the windows was done towards the end of this period, in the fifteenth and early sixteenth century. By 1400, however, the village had a church of the same dimensions and general external appearance as it has today. Inside, of course, it looked vastly different, with the rood loft, altars, images and lights, associated with the liturgy and teaching of the medieval church. The nave was also spared the clutter of the modern pews.

Appledore and the surrounding villages were left festering with discontent throughout the fifteenth century. The whole of this area was a strong centre of what was styled Lollardry by those who were anxious to suppress this way of thinking. John Wyclif started the movement in the reign of Richard II. In his early days he denounced the excessive interest of the bishops in "temporalities". They filled the high offices of state instead of looking after their dioceses. He also inveighed against the wealth of the monastic orders which could have been better spent on the poor parish clergy. Though he was not actively involved in Wat Tyler's rising, his doctrines played some part in the movement. As time went on, he was much more engaged with doctrine, for example, he believed that in the sacrament, whilst the elements were undoubtedly the body and blood of Christ, they retained the substance of bread and wine—consubstantiation in contrast to transubstantiation. In practice some of his followers probably retained some of his earlier "levelling" ideas, though they were persecuted in the main not for them but for their non-conformist views on doctrine which made them heretics in the eyes of the church authorities. For that reason it was the church rather than the civil power which harried them.

The earliest evidence of Lollardry in this neighbourhood is in 1428 when the Archbishop charged twenty-six people from villages which included Tenterden and Woodchurch (but not Appledore) and got some of them imprisoned, others hanged or burnt at the stake. In 1431 the vicar of Appledore was ordered to put heretics to penance in the parish church of Appledore. Nine years later a man called Alan Elys of Tenterden was executed for treason. One of his quarters was hung on the pillory at Appledore. Evidently, it was then felt that the village needed a warning of the dangers of opposing Church or State. That did not stop riots taking place in Appledore in 1450 and 1456. Active resistance by the Lollards was, however, by then dying out and, though non-conformity continued, it took other forms.

What is not entirely clear is the part which Appledore played in Jack Cade's rising in 1450. This movement was quite different from Wat Tyler's. It was not a Peasants' Revolt. Indeed it included a considerable number of the gentry, as well as large numbers of village tradesmen. The main motives of those who joined the movement seems to have been their anger at the undoubted misgovernment of the country under the feeble rule of Henry VI, and their even greater resentment at the peculations of the chief agents of the government in Kent. Of these the most notorious was James Fiennes, Lord Saye and Sele, then sheriff of the county. Like Wat Tyler's men, Jack Cade's forces were successful in seizing the City of London, and could have taken over the government. As it was, the rebellion collapsed, through bad leadership, on July 6th, only a few weeks after the outbreak had started at the end of May.

One reason why the rebellion was so quickly repressed was the conciliatory policy of the two archbishops, who at the time were the King's advisers. They not only counselled him to grant wholesale pardons (and, unlike Richard II) to honour them, but also induced him to enquire into some of the undoubted grievances and to remedy them. These pardons, which name many of the men in the different village contingents, are a valuable source of village history. Oddly, Appledore is one of the few villages which is not mentioned in the list. Stone, Ebony, Wittersham, Kenardington, Romney, Snargate, Brookland all secured pardons for their part in the rebellion up to July 7th. There were none for Appledore.

Appledore, however, had taken part in the rebellion. The riot in the village, already mentioned, must have been connected with it, and we know from the pardon obtained by one Appledore man, rather more about this or another similar incident. "John Claydych, late of Apuldre, laborer", obtained his pardon on October 16th, 1451. Together with other Kentish men he was paraded before Henry VI at Blackheath. All of them were naked to the waist and had to stand with ropes round their necks—to "submit to the King's grace". July 7th, 1450, was the date of the collapse of the rebellion and the general pardon. John Claydych was pardoned for all his offences between that date and February 1451, and in particular for "having with other traitors unknown, of the society of William Parmenter, who called himself the second Captain of Kent, plotted the King's death and destruction of the realm, having congregated at Apuldre and elsewhere in Kent on August 31st, 1450, to the number of 200 men, and levied war in Kent until February 6th, 1451". Parmenter's armed assembly at Appledore was near the Windmill, probably Horne's Mill. This we know from the entry in the Rye records "Paid 8d. to a certain soldier called Robert by name to go to Apuldore to make enquiry whether the captain with his army who was then near the windmill there had entered that town or not."

William Parmenter, of Faversham, was not the only follower of Cade who continued resistance after the general pardon of July 6th, 1450, had caused most of the rebels to submit. Appledore's absence from the general pardon suggests that John Claydych and other Appledore men had carried on the struggle rather longer, and not that Appledore had refused to join the rebellion. There is no evidence that Parmenter was imbued with Lollardry, but some of the other "captains" who carried on the resistance after Jack Cade's death undoubtedly were, and they were indeed indicted for being heretics

21

and Lollards as well as for active rebellion. Appledore's part in Jack Cade's rising was certainly only one symptom of the unrest in the village during the first half of the fifteenth century which, without any doubt, was connected with Lollardry.

The family of Horne continued to flourish in Appledore throughout this period, owning land in other villages as well. William Horne, the Commissioner for suppressing the 1381 rebellion, may be buried under the chest tomb in the south chapel in Appledore church. Sir Henry Horne, possibly his son, of Hornes Place, Kenardington and of Appledore, sat in Parliament in 1404 as one of the Knights of the Shire for Kent, and was made Sheriff of the County in 1406. Robert Horne of Kenardington and Hornes Place, Appledore, was sheriff in 1452 and Knight of the Shire in 1460. This marked the peak of the family's distinction, but they always remained great landowners and well connected with the local county families. Gervase Horne, who seems to have been in trouble for rebellion in 1470, died in 1493, and an elaborate enquiry in 1496 into his land-holdings shows that he held a thousand acres overall in a number of parishes including Kenardington. Hasted says that the family bought the Manor of Kenardington in 1533, but he seems a bit confused because he also says that they moved to Kenardington in the reign of Henry VII (1485-1509) on buying the manor to which they gave their name. What seems clear is that in the early sixteenth century, the family who already owned land in Kenardington, acquired the manor there, including the manor house, which from then on was known as Little Hornes. Whether or not they actually lived in their old home at Hornes Place, Appledore, they continued to own it up to the accession of Queen Elizabeth. The family, however, though wealthy and well connected, no longer produced any men of distinction. This may not have been for any lack of talent but because they had supported the House of York in the Wars of the Roses. Edward IV gave a pension to the widow of the Horne who died fighting on the Yorkist side at Towton.

Other people were also doing quite well. The monks of Canterbury, as Lords of the Manor, continued their policy of inning the marsh, and two large inclosures were made. Five hundred and sixty-six acres were walled in in 1400, another 600 in 1477. This last inning is identified as part of the great marsh of Appledore called Ketesflete. The addition of these considerable acres of fertile land produced a proportionate increase in the wealth of the parish. Trade also continued to have the use of the seaway, called in a document of 1407 the Apoldreflete, running, it says, from the sea to Bodiam. By then almost certainly the channel entered the sea at Rye. Trade and agriculture flourished to the extent of making a number of the parishioners people of some substance. They had at any rate enough cash and chattels to make it worth their while to make wills to dispose of this property, and, from 1400 onwards, the number of

wills of people living in Appledore which still survive is quite
remarkable. In the first half of the period covered in this chapter
down to 1500 there are some 30 wills, in the second down to 1558
some 100.

The earliest, made in 1410, is of an Appledore man, John de
Gosborne, son of Thomas de Gosborne of Appledore, who moved to
London and evidently prospered there. He had a mansion in Aldgate
and left legacies of over £35, including one pound for the church of
Appledore in which his father and mother were buried. His family
continued to live in the parish. Andrew Gosborne (who leaves out the
"de") in his will of 1463 made bequests of parcels of land called
"Tenacrys" and "Five fardinges".

A number of these earlier wills show that the testators held land,
which would pass to their heirs by the custom of the manor, as well
as the money and chattels which they disposed of in their will. They
are evidence of the emergence of yeomen, small farmers and tradesmen in the parish, of a far higher standard of living than that of the
labourers who made up the greater part of the population.

In this earlier period the practice started of making bequests for
what may be broadly described as the spiritual advantage of the
testator's soul. William Catelotte in 1483 left land called Old Fish-
cokkes in Kenardington for a priest to sing in the chapel of our Lady
in Appledore. Isabella Perye's will of 1465 is the apogee of this type
of bequest: "And all the residue to dispose of to the high pleasure
and worship of God and to the benefyte of my sowle, my hosbondes,
my fader, my moder and all cristen sowles, or elles some goo to scala
celi and atte other stacyonys aboute Rome, where as pleyne remission
and delyvringe sowlys out of peyne is had". Others provided for less
spiritual but more practical needs: "Four shirts for four poor men for
four shillings" and for mending the causeway between the high cross
in the market and the Rhee. Bequests for making up the road were to
continue for many centuries. It didn't need T.I.R. lorries to churn
the street into a quagmire.

Two wills of this period, incidentally, show that, in addition to the
parish church, there was in 1470 a chapel of St. James on the Heath,
and in 1495 a hermit there.

From 1500 to 1558 the number of wills increases rapidly. They
are mainly of interest as giving the names of those living here, and
some field names. From some a glimpse of life in Appledore at the
time emerges.

An attempt was evidently made in 1519 to set up a grammar
school in the village. In that year William Brokhill, evidently a rich
man, since his legacies total £180, made elaborate provision to secure
an annual payment of £8 in perpetuity. This was to pay the salary of
a priest to assist in the church on Sundays, where he was to sing plain
song in the choir, and on working days to teach grammar to boys at a

school to be established in the street. For this he made special provision. Part of the residue of his estate was to be applied in buying "some convenient house or shop as near the church as possible". How far this venture succeeded is not recorded. The school is not mentioned in any later document. The place intended could be what is now the bakery.

Lydd records record one feature of Appledore life in this period. A fair amount of money was spent by Lydd on providing entertainment and the accounts record the payments made to the players who performed. Some were well-known companies like the King's or Lord Arundel's players. Others came from neighbouring villages. Appledore provided players in 1488, 1516 and 1517. They were paid as much as 32/9d. on the last occasion.

Several wills give some picture of what the market place looked like at the time. There was a high cross and near it a "lake", or what in later documents is called a horsepit—presumably a pond. In 1523 William Marshall, the vicar of the day and a man of considerable private wealth bequeathed £40 to provide a conduit of running water to the market. Whether this was actually built we do not know. William Marshal, evidently, saw some inclination on the part of the people of Appledore to take their time. He expressly provided that if the work was not done in eighteen months, the legacy should lapse, or be applied to mending the roadway. If that, in turn, was not done in three years, then the money was to be spent for the benefit of his soul!

All the roads were foul. Testators in Appledore, as in many other parishes, left money for their repair. Appledore wills provide time and again for particular sections of the road to be repaired "from the smith's door towards the marsh", "between the church and the parsonage barn", "between the Leys and the town", "between the Heath and the Gatehouse". It was clearly an endless job.

The manor documents also throw some light on progress in the village. From 1464 onwards there are a number of leases of "shambles" in the street. The leases are of small plots of anything between 15 and 19 ft. in depth, and frontages of 5 to 9 feet. These seem to have been sites for moveable stalls, if that is the right interpretation of "shamels". These were placed between the highway "regia strata" and a small footway "via pedile" leading to the church. It rather looks as though all these stalls were placed on what is now the grass between the roadway and the still surviving footpath to the church. Clearly there was no basis at this time for any claim by the local authority, as there is now, to be the owner of this area! They were the property of the manor.

The market area did not consist entirely of these booths on the east side of the street. On the other side of the street there are several references to shops, and indeed a will of 1469 refers to the "long house that is to say the shoppe". This could possibly be the present bakery.

24

All this development of the weekly market was deliberate policy by the manor. They stood to gain by the increase in the market tolls, and from the rents they got from the traders for the lease of their pitches. In some cases the lease was granted on condition of the trader repairing an existing shamble or building a new one at his own cost.

Throughout this period the church was the great centre of life in the village, and the parishioners endowed it generously. In their wills they provided for its needs—altar cloths, chalices and the furnishing of the rood-loft. In particular, many legacies were given for keeping the lights burning over the shrines of the numerous saints represented in the church. Ten saints are mentioned in wills as having lights. In addition to the lights of the high altar and of the Rood, there were lights for Our Ladie of Pitie (our Lady holding the crucified body of Our Lord), St Catherine, St Stephen, St Margaret, St Christopher, St Barbara, St Nicholas, St George, St Anthony and St Erasmus. There were also chapels on the Heath, another at Reading Street and the Chapel of St Mary at Ebony. Two new windows were made in the south aisle in this period. Thomas Knelle in 1510 left 66/8d. to provide a new window "next to that Robert Clerk made". John Skele in 1520 left 33/4d. for a new chalice, John Clarke in 1522 a salt of silver and gilt for the same purpose. The effect of this rich endowment must have been most impressive. The lights would all have been burning, before the images of the saints, before the Rood, on the high altar, and the altars of our Lady of Pitie, St Margaret and St Erasmus. Behind the rood was the rood loft, painted with scenes of the crucifixion, reached by a staircase up to the entrance still to be seen in the chancel wall. In many of the windows of this time, and as late as 1700, there was stained glass. In the east window one of the Priors of Dover, patrons of the church, was depicted at prayer. In the south chapel the window showed St Catherine, with the Emperor Maximine in hell "fastened to such a wheel as he had put her to death upon". In the north aisle you saw the Virgin as Queen of Heaven, and in other windows John Horne, and a parishioner of this period called Wolbold. There was light and colour everywhere. The walls were painted. Fragments of a George and Dragon still survive. Great changes in the ornament and decoration of the church were soon to be made in the reign of Edward VI and, after a respite in Queen Mary's time, under Queen Elizabeth.

Changes were also to be made in the administration of the church and of the Manor land. In 1534 Henry VIII had repudiated the authority of Rome, and two years later his first action under the Reformation, the dissolution of the Monasteries, began. Parliament gave the necessary authority in 1536, but, even before this, Dover Priory had come to an end. For some years it had been in decay, and in 1535 it was suppressed. Its long patronage of the church of Appledore and its land holdings reverted to the Archbishop of Canterbury, Thomas Cranmer.

25

The Priory of Canterbury survived as long as any, but in 1540 it also was suppressed and its ownership of the Manor of Appledore passed to the newly appointed Dean and Chapter. A new era had begun for Appledore.

PLATE 1
Horne's Place - a sketch made in 1857

PLATE 2
Horne's Place Chapel

PLATE 3
The Street, Appledore, looking south.

PLATE 4
The ancient long house, a sketch made in 1799

PLATE 5

The long house as it is today, comprising the Bakery, the Craft Shop
and three other dwellings.

PLATE 6

Appledore Church. Photograph of the interior, taken in 1870, showing
the tie beams in the chancel before their removal by Vicar Russell. Note
Vicar Kirby's pulpit and reading desk, also the Royal Arms behind the
Pulpit.

PLATE 7
Ambrose Cogger's map of the Chute Estate in 1628

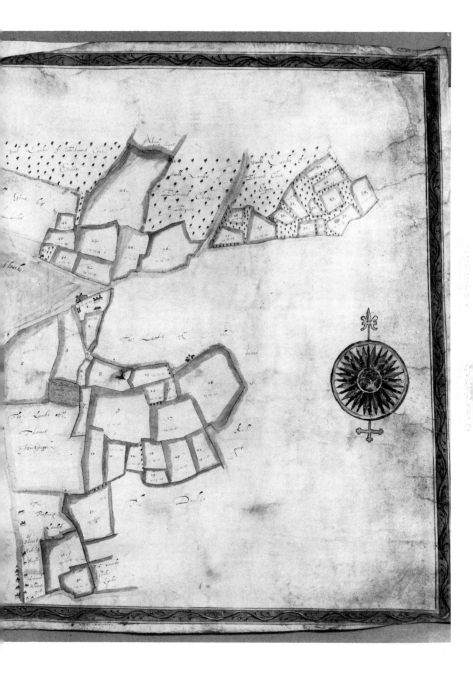

PLATE 8
The Union Mill on the Heath, demolished in 1877.

PLATE 9
Court Lodge, demolished about 1885.
The sketch made in 1852 does not show the remains of
the early 15th century house still surviving in the interior.

About 1890

PLATE 10
The old Red Lion in 1890, the landlord, Barney Noakes,
at the door and the Jubilee bus which ran from Tenterden to the station.

APPLEDORE CHURCH, KENT.

PLATE 11
Appledore Church, from the South-East - sketch by R. S. Miles, 1845.

PLATE 12 The nave and part of the south aisle during the excavations in 1925, with Dr. Cock holding a pickaxe.

PLATE 13 Interior of the church today.

THE TUDORS AND THE LATE 17th CENTURY

The Chutes replace the Hornes—Changes in land management by the Manor—Absentee landlords—The farmers of Court Lodge Farm

The new era in Appledore opened with the disappearance of the Hornes, the only aristocratic family ever to live long in the parish and with the introduction of a new system of land management by the new lords of the Manor, the Dean and Chapter of Canterbury. The Hornes had probably transferred most of their interest from Appledore to Kenardington after Roger Horne acquired the manor of Kenardington in 1533. The family became Lords of the Manor and patrons of the church of Kenardington, with the right of appointing the vicar. Probably from then on they lost most of their interest in Appledore. No member of the family is recorded in the Appledore Registers, the transcripts of which begin in 1563. What is not clear is whether they moved from Hornes Place, Appledore, to Little Hornes, Kenardington, in 1533 or later. When Roger Horne died in 1544 he owned not only his manor of Kenardington, but also five dwelling houses of which one, clearly Hornes Place, Appledore, was held of the Dean and Chapter of Canterbury. His son Henry succeeded to all the property and, on his death in 1565, left all his estate to his daughter Benet. She was to be the last of the Hornes of Appledore and Kenardington. She became a recusant, one of those who refused to take the oath of allegiance to Queen Elizabeth, and in 1570, at the age of eleven, fled to the continent without the Queen's licence. She married another recusant, Richard Guildeforde. They both died in exile, he in 1586, she in 1597. There were no children and the long line of the Hornes of Appledore ended with her death.

Another potentate had arrived in the parish, Philip Chute. A man of distinction and of great wealth, he belonged to a family of eminence, of which Chaloner Chute of the Vyne, near Basingstoke, a distinguished lawyer and Speaker of the House of Commons at the time of the Restoration, was to be the most prominent member. Philip Chute had won fame and the gratitude of Henry VIII at the siege of Boulogne on September 14th, 1544. Here he had served as standard bearer to the men of arms of the Kings Band. He was rewarded with the grant of a canton to his coat of arms—the lion of England on a field argent and vert—and with considerable wealth. He had already been given the confiscated monasteries at Winchelsea and Faversham. The King, on July 15th, 1545, appointed him Captain of Camber Castle and, more to the point, provided with the appointment a

27

salary of 2/- a day, and the right to draw 6d. a day for each man on an establishment of eight "souldeors" and six "gonners". Henry VIII's patent was endorsed later on behalf of Queen Mary and Queen Elizabeth, thus ensuring the continued payment of the pension.

Philip Chute undoubtedly owned the lease of, and lived in, Hornes Place, Appledore, and was buried in Appledore church. When he acquired it is not known. Hasted is wrong in saying that when Richard Guildeforde and his wife Benet, the daughter of Henry Horne, were attainted, Hornes Place, with his other property, was confiscated to the crown "and the Queen soon afterwards granted to Philip Chute Hornes Place and its lands, who afterwards resided here". Henry Horne did not die till 1565, only two years before Philip Chute's death, and there is no reason to think that he was a recusant or that his property was confiscated. His daughter Benet was then only six years old and was not declared a recusant till 1570. The legend of the Queen bestowing the property of the Papist recusant on her father's gallant standard bearer is much more colourful, but on his own statement he acquired Hornes Place by purchase, and did so probably some considerable time before Henry Horne died in 1565.

Philip Chute was buried in Appledore church on April 7th, 1567. He had made his will in March 1565 and it was proved in February 1568. It shows the considerable amount of property which he owned. His holdings included land in Iden, Appledore, Kenardington and elsewhere in Kent "which I bought of John Harper, gent". He possessed the manor of Herste and other lands in Godmersham and Chilham and land in Bethersden. In Sussex he owned land not only in Iden, as already mentioned, but also in Brede and Sedlescombe. All this property was divided between his three sons, all still under 21. His personal chattels went to his sons and his two daughters. George, his eldest son, amongst other chattels was given "all household stuff in my house of Horne at Appledore".

Appledore got little enough out of this great estate—nothing except 6d. to "every pore person that shall come to my burial and ask for God's sake". On the other hand he claimed in his will the right to be buried in "my chapel in the parish church of Appledore" and "to have a tombstone over me declaring the certain day and tyme when God called me to his mercy". He was duly buried in the south chapel on April 7th, 1567. This is recorded in the transcript of the Parish Registers which survives in the Cathedral Library at Canterbury. No tombstone seems to have been put over him, or, if it was, it has been removed. In 1925, when Dr. Cock was restoring the south chapel, he found that an earlier burial had been displaced, when a brick vault had been made in the floor of the chapel to hold the coffin of Jeffery Munk, who died in 1817, and his third wife. From this burial only a jawbone and a few other fragments remained. These were gathered and piously reinterred under the window where the altar in the chapel now stands. On the reasonable assumption that they were the mortal remains of Henry VIII's standard bearer, Dr. Cock had an inscription carved fulfilling as far as possible Philip Chute's wish, recording the day and year of his burial, the day of his death not being known. Unfortunately the year is incorrectly recorded as 1566.

The fact that Philip Chute claimed the south chapel as "his" suggests that the Hornes had made a similar claim, based, possibly, on their assumption of a liability to maintain and embellish it.

Philip Chute's son George almost certainly never lived in Hornes Place or elsewhere in Appledore, nor did any other later member of the family. No baptism, marriage or burial of the family is recorded in the registers. His father's will provided that none of the farmers of his lands were to be disturbed during his son's minority. Almost certainly the Chutes who had moved to Bethersden treated their Appledore lands as one of their outlying estates, and Hornes Place became the farmhouse of one of their tenants. There is a reference in an inquest in Canterbury in 1590 which tells of a house near Appledore, decayed and wasted. This may refer to the place, but the identification is not certain. If the reference to Hornes Place is correct some interesting facts emerge. The chief witness, Stephen Cowper, says that the house was already decayed and wasted by 1587, when it was occupied by a man called Broughton, who was succeeded by a man called Thomas Adams. This would be consistent with the theory that after Philip Chute's death, Hornes Place rapidly reverted to a farmhouse. Stephen Cowper, incidentally, is recorded as having fled the realm without licence in 1587, and it is possible that he was the steward of the property who went to join his old employer in exile, but later returned to England.

The Chutes remained non-resident landlords in Appledore for many years after Philip Chute's death. A very handsome estate map made for the family was discovered by Dr. Cock in a cupboard in the Sessions House at Maidstone. A photograph of this is on the centre page of this book. This shows all the fields owned in 1628 by Edward Chute of Bethersden, Esquire. It is now preserved in the County Archives Office. The 76 parcels of land totalled 570 acres. In addition Edward Chute owned considerable woodland in Herons Wood. The land included all the fields round Hornes Place to the east and west of the Ashford road, apart from what is now Gusborne farm. This block included the mill (shown on the map) the mound of which still remains, as does the lane leading to it which is also marked on the map. He owned some land on both sides of Moor Lane and—the largest block—on both sides of the Tenterden road beyond the crossroads right as far as the present Tenterden and Reading sewers. All this land was very suitable to let to farming tenants. Unfortunately none of the field names are shown. These would have been given in the book mentioned in the legend at the top of the map.

The Chutes and their successors held this land down to 1882. The departure of the Hornes and the arrival of the Chutes made little difference to the inhabitants of Appledore. Philip Chute lived at Hornes Place and requested that he be buried in the church. His descendants lived in Bethersden only two parishes away, and the farm land continued to be let to good substantial farmers, as indeed it had in the time of the Hornes.

The manor, however, made many changes during this period in their system for managing their land, which was virtually all the land in the rest of the parish. Up to the end of the medieval period the demesne land had been farmed by the manor and the farming profits went into the coffers of the monks at Canterbury. The farm work was organised by the Manor's Bailiff from Court Lodge. The work was done partly by the Manor's serfs, partly by the forced labour which the tenants of the other land on the manor had to give as a condition of their tenancy. Serfdom was abolished by the end of the 15th century and it got progressively harder to get the free tenants to work on the manor farm. The manor had to change its system and let the demesne—the manor or Court Lodge farm—to a substantial tenant paying a full rent for his tenancy. When this important change was made is not certain. The Court Lodge had been burned down at the start of the sixteenth century. Thomas Goldstone, Prior from 1495 to 1517 rebuilt it. Almost at once, in 1513, it became only the occasional office of the Bailiff, where he collected his rents and held the manor courts - the "Curia" of the Manor. The lodge's main use from then on was to be the farmhouse of the tenant of Court Lodge Farm. The first recorded tenant was William Brokhill of Appledore, yeoman. He secured a large and valuable holding. The Court Lodge was next to, if not in the same class as Hornes Place, the most important house in the village and, in the absence of any resident gentry, its occupant the most important personality in the parish. Court Lodge had a hall and a parlour and at least two bedrooms, one with six bedsteads in it. The demesne land and the manor mill were part of the lease. William Brokhill also got a large part of the East Marsh and part of the Becard. Two other holdings came to him; 195 acres recently inned in the Marsh called Cow Leas, and 63 acres of saltings. The other holding was 118 acres in Shirley Moor, newly drained and cultivated. For all this he paid an annual rent starting at £46 14s. 9d. rising to £51 13s. 9d. He played a leading part in village life. His will, providing for a school in Appledore, has already been mentioned and it directed that he should be buried in the church.

The Manor retained its manorial rents and dues, also the whole of the Appledore channel "and the profits of the traders using it". The tenant had to allow the lodge to used for the business of the manor court. The lease was, furthermore, for a fixed term of years. Whether or not the new appointment was associated with the change of policy, some thirty years before the Prior of Canterbury had created a new offical to manage

30

the manor. His office was that of "Bedell" and John Pote of Canterbury was the first to hold it, in 1477. In 1498 he was given a house and gar-den in Appledore, bounded on the south "by the Kings Weir "regia gurges" called the channel".

In 1527 the lease of Court Lodge and all the lands let to William Brokhill was granted to John Asshele for 19 years at the increased rent of £55 2s. 9d. He was expressly required to maintain the channel and to collect and hand over the payments from the ships and traders using it. This clause in the lease was repeated in all the leases which followed, long after the channel had become unusable except for shallow draft wherries. There is, however, no doubt whatever that the channel carried ships (large by the standards of the day) well into the fifteenth century. Thus in 1445 the Corporation of Lydd "paid 10d. for the breakfast of the men going to Appledore for the ship hired to escort the Lady Margaret who is to be Queen of England". There are later entries in these accounts, about the making of a harbour there (in 1468 and 1488). As late as 1582 Dover was paying freight for timber carried by water from Newenden and Appledore to Rye.

One of the first acts of the Dean and Chapter of Canterbury after taking over the manor from the Prior was to appoint Stephen Thorneherste of Canterbury to be Receiver and Beadel of the Manor. Simultaneously he became their tenant of Fairfield and part of the Court Lodge land. The Court Lodge was not let to him. The house he got was the parsonage of Fairfield. In return he was required "to find an able priest to sing or say divine service at times right and con-venient" in Fairfield church. Court Lodge and the main part of the demesne continued to be let to a well-to-do yeoman farmer. Stephen Thorneherste would have collected his first rents from Giles Ascherinden. His father, buried in Appledore church in 1538, had held Manor Farm before him. Richard Ashenden who died in 1569 was a later tenant, to be succeeded by his son William. One yeoman succeeded another, living in and taking a full part in the life of the village.

A further, far reaching, change in the Manor's land management system was soon to be made. No longer would the Dean and Chapter give tenancies to working farmers. Instead they leased the Manor Farm to members of the nobility and gentry, leaving them the task of sub-letting the farm to working tenants. William Ashenden, gentleman, was granted a lease in 1582 for 21 years at a rent of £59 2s. 9d. a year. Whether he was a working tenant is not clear, but he was, within a year, in 1583, to hold his land from a much more eminent occupier, Queen Elizabeth herself. Unfortunately, the original deed, recording the acquisition by the Queen of the lease of the manor, was sold to buyers in America. Two facts emerge from the text. The lease to Queen Elizabeth was granted, on payment of £500, for 40 years at the existing rent of £59, sweetened every ten years by a bonus of £100. Secondly it is known that the Dean and Chapter at first resisted the Queen's request and were evidently put in their place, for a letter written to Walsingham, the Queen's secretary, explains that the Dean and Chapter had taken their stand not through " obstinacy but respect for their statutes".

Queen Elizabeth did not keep her interest in Appledore for very long. Within four years her lease was transferred to Thomas Diggs of London, Esquire.

This Thomas Diggs was almost certainly the very distinguished member of the Barham family of that name who had done excellent work as a comissioner for repairing Dover Harbour in 1586, and had gone on to become muster-master-general of the forces serving in the Netherlands in 1586. He was also commissioned to fit out a fleet to explore the dominions of the Cham of Cathay. In the process he had acquired great wealth, and some of this he was now investing in Appledore. This was all very nice and convenient for the Dean and Chapter but it meant that the greater part of the land in Appledore was now held by an even remoter landlord, interested only in the rents he could get from his sub-tenants. By 1618 the lease passed to the great Culpepper family and by 1680 to the Hulse family who held it till 1888.

The introduction of absentee landlords (in law tenants but in practice landlords) was to go still further. Court Lodge farm was not the only land affected by the change. The 1628 map shows a number of persons holding land of the Manor apart from the Chutes.
They were :

Sir Edward Hales, Bart., descendant of Sir Robert Hales who was beheaded on Tower Hill by Wat Tyler in 1381. Sir Edward took the Parliamentary side in the Civil War. He lived in Tenterden.

Sir Anthony Mayney of Linton, whose grandson spent the whole family fortune in supporting Charles I.

Sir Edward Radcliffe, physician to James I, whose family seat was at Hitchin, Herts, but who also owned property at Sevington near Willesborough.

John Moyle, of Kenardington Manor, who was, like Edward Chute, at least a local landowner.

Finally there was Sir Francis Fane, two years earlier created first Earl of Westmorland.

Two, and only two, of the landowners shown on the map actually lived in the parish. "Knell Gent" is almost certainly James Knell of Appledore, Gent, whose will, proved in 1627 provided that his lands were to be sold for the benefit of his children, and who was a member of a family which had lived in Appledore since at least 1526. "Woolball, Gent", is Robert Woolball of Appledore, gent, whose will was proved in 1650. His name also had appeared for many years in Appledore records.

The new policy gave the Dean and Chapter an easy way out of their responsibilities as landowners—so far as Court Lodge farm was concerned. So it did at first for the other holdings. All the notable families holding the leases mentioned above were, in 1646, still paying their quit rents to the Dean and Chapter of Canterbury. This is shown by the entries in the book kept by the Manor's rent collector. None of them appear in the 1768 return. Somewhere between these dates the Manor had again to lease their land to working farmers.

Other manors had the same experience. The financial return to a Lord of the Manor was getting far less profitable. As is clear from later chapters, the Dean and Chapter's record was among the less brilliant.

6

SOCIAL DEVELOPMENTS
After the Reformation and in the 17th Century

For the social history of the village during this period the main
sources of information are the Archdeacon's visitations (in so far as
they survive), the transcripts of the registers which start from 1563,
wills and property deeds.

One feature of life of which something can be gathered from the
wills and visitations is the change in religious attitudes and practices
as the result of the Reformation. Henry VIII had been content with
abolishing the jurisdiction of the Pope and dissolving the monasteries.
The latter step had the effect in Appledore of transferring the
ownership of the manor from the Prior and Monks of Canterbury to
the Dean and Chapter. So far as religious practice was concerned,
Henry would allow no change in the liturgy, and the clergy were
required to remain celibate. Archbishop Cranmer, who had beaten
the gun, had to conceal his wife, and the unfortunate woman, when
she travelled round with him, had to be carried in a box. Legacies to
endow the lights before the altar tend to die out, but at least one
will (Thos Shoeberry's) in 1544 makes such provision, and some lights
still burned before the altars in the church. All this changed with the
accession of Edward VI in 1547. In 1548 the marriage of the clergy
was legalised by statute. A year later the mass was prohibited by law,
and the Act of Uniformity was passed. In 1550 an order was made
that stone altars were to be taken down. In that year the Vicar of
Appledore, amongst others, was hailed before the Archdeacon and
testified that the old service books had been done away with.
Meanwhile images, lights and any ornaments unacceptable to the
doctrine of the reformed church laid down by Cranmer were
removed. There is an account of the sale of a cross of silver and gilt
weighing 3 lb. and a pair of censers weighing 3¼ lb., for a total of
19/4d. Queen Mary, of course, reversed all this. The old liturgy was
restored in 1553, the first year of her reign. Next year married clergy
were expelled from their benefices unless they agreed to be separated
from their wives. Stone altars were ordered to be set up again on pain
of a fine of £100.

All this must have been extremely confusing for the people and
clergy. The Archdeacon's visitation in 1557 during the last year of
Queen Mary's reign, ordered the vicar, John Kytching, who had
been instituted the year before, to "cause the faces of the images in

34

the windows that be blotted to be made clean", to provide furnishings for the altar, vestments, and "a fair mass book". It rather looks as though he or his predecessor had not caught up with the restoration of the old liturgy by Queen Mary. A fragment of the old mass book certified in 1550 as done away with "abolitus" possibly survives. Dr Cock found in the backing of some deeds belonging to one of the churchwardens serving in 1553 two strips of parchment cut with a razor. Together they form half a sheet of a mass book and give the liturgy for the sixth and seventh Sundays after Whitsun. The fragment is still in good condition, the rubrics have kept their colour, and the text is easily legible. As was customary it was "pricked" with the notes of the chant in the portions to be sung by the priest, though he must have had good eyesight to make them out. The lettering is evidence that the book must have been used for many centuries.

In 1558 Queen Elizabeth came to the throne and John Kytching and the congregation of Appledore had soon to adapt themselves once more to the practices of the Reformed Protestant Church of England, which were to be observed from then onwards to the present time. In 1559 Queen Elizabeth's Parliament passed a new Act of Uniformity, penalties were laid down for celebrating mass, compulsory attendance at the reformed service of the church was ordained and once again the clergy were free to marry.

John Kytching took advantage of the new dispensation and in June 1568, twelve years after he had been appointed vicar of Appledore, he took out a licence to marry Joan Gunter, the widow of William Gunter of Appledore, and the mother of a number of children. Alas, only six months later, on December 16th, he was in a bad way. Such was his condition that he could not sign the will which he then made, leaving all his possessions to her. He lingered another two months. Then he died and was buried. His widow's further adventures shed light on the consequences of adapting the clergy to married life. In October 1569 she was charged at the Archdeacon's Court for withholding, as executrix of Thomas Betts or Bell of Faversham, 40/- bequeathed by him to the poor of Appledore.

Worse still, a charge was laid that Mr. William Russell, vicar of Preston near Faversham, "and Joan Kitchen keep house together, have been asked (i.e. banns called) these nine weeks and not yet married". The latter irregularity was put right on October 26th, when the two were married at Appledore. All other charges were wiped from the book, one hopes, when poor Joan Russell died a few days later and was buried on November 1st.

The Archdeacon's visitation dealt with a number of matters. It enquired into the state of the fabric of the church, and the conduct of the clergy. It found out and recorded the number of parishioners receiving the sacrament, and dealt with any charges of failing to attend church services. Finally it listened to complaints of moral failings— mostly, but not exclusively, breaches of the seventh commandment.

35

Cases of failure to attend service on Sunday are not very frequent. Fines, of course, could be and were sometimes exacted. Millers seem to have been the target in the early seventeenth century. In 1628 "William Standley, late miller of the towne mill of Appledore and now miller of Tenterden" was charged with "Gryndinge upon the Sabbath daye". He successfully pleaded that his "gryndinge was at the special request of the inhabitants of Appledore by reason of the not goeing and gryndinge of the mill, detected of a long tyme before, who did exceedingly want bred". And "seeinge that the wynd did then serve very fitlye", he set the mill going. Three years later the wrath of the church turned on Joseph Comfort the water miller—evidently there was a water mill as well as the windmills at Court Lodge and Hornes. Joseph Comfort successfully pleaded that, unless he set his mill going, much land would be flooded. That was all he did, he said, on Sundays "unless perchance sometimes he set by his mill and look on it". The contemplative water miller seems to have set about getting his own back on the church. Next year he was in court again for "abusing the churchyard with his basones out of his window as is too manifest to be seene and smelt". He pleaded that it was his "maides negligence and fault". The court's verdict is not recorded. Meanwhile in the same year another parishioner, Nicholas George, was in trouble for profaning the Sabbath by "goeing a fisheing". He pleaded that he *had* gone to evening service, and as for his absence in the morning "by mere chance some marshes had been dreened " (=drowned =flooded) and "a great store of fish was then to be had which if the same had not been saved it had been lost". The result of the impeccable logic of his plea is also not recorded.

Some of the investigations into private morals are distressing reading, some amusing. Joan Russell was not the only parishioner brought to the Archdeacon for failing to distribute legacies for the benefit of the parish or individual parishioners. The court was often a convenient means of bring pressure to bear on dilatory or dishonest executors. There are also orders made to prevent victualling during the hours of divine service. In 1580 drunkenness is the principle target of the Court. Thomas Hudeswell had "abused the creature of God, viz, beer". Anthony Remnaunte "doth keep his house in a disordered manner in drinking in an excessive manner and allowing others to do the same". Mathew Whatlowe frequents the tavern "and then drinketh more than is sufficient"—and so on.

In 1596 the churchwardens decided to regulate the seating of the congregation. Men sat with women but the younger members of the flock were put in front, the older "more able to bear charge" at the back. The change now made involved some changes in the seating order. None resisted except the wife of Thomas Berrie. This was unpopular with her new "seat fellows". She went back to her old seat where the men told her to get out and so "she removed again to another seat thus flitting from place to place to the trouble of the parishioners".

36

One very curious incursion of the Archdeacon took place in 1662. In that year William Reskur was brought before him for "practicing chirugery without licence".

Concern with the seventh commandment varied from decade to decade. In the surviving records the first instance is in 1557 and they go on steadily till the start of the seventeenth century when they get less frequent, though the number of fatherless children baptised do not. What penalties were exacted for those whose offence was proven is not given. In a much earlier period, in the last years of the thirteenth century, the penalties were brutal. The guilty parties were flogged round the church. At Lympne a knight, Thomas de Marynes, was found guilty of the offence. Because it was "not thought decent" for a knight to do public penance, he got away with a fine of 20 marks. One of the ladies involved was ordered to be flogged five times round the market place and five times round the church "in camisia ut moris est" dressed, as is the custom, in her chemise or shift. The penalty was reduced as time went on to doing public penance in church before the congregation. This penalty, including the appearance "in a white sheet" was enforced in Appledore as late as 1727.

The Archdeacon's visitation, of course, concentrated a lot of attention on the fabric of the church, and the performance of their duties by the clergy. As early as 1511 it was found that the chancel was not being repaired. It was in decay again in 1560 through the default of the farmer of the Parsonage. These failures of the farmer were to become a recurrent complaint. They all derived from the practice of successive Archbishops in appointing as Vicars wealthy clergy, who rarely, if ever, visited the parish. These absentee vicars leased the vicarage and the glebe to a farmer , i.e. to a tenant. The tenant, as a condition of his lease, was responsible for the upkeep of the chancel and, it would seem, of the churchyard. Typical absentee vicars were John King, who held the benefice from 1568-1576, but lived at Canterbury or Windsor, in both of which places he was a Canon. From 1576-90 there was a resident vicar, George Bassett. One of his appearances before the Archdeacon's Court in 1579 gives an account of the sanitary arrangements in Appledore. He reported that he had enclosed with a railing a small strip of land next to the vicarage on which for many years it had been the practice to lay what today goes into the sewers, "lying there very indecently and unhandsomely and in open sight of all the parishioners then resorting usually to church".

He was followed by a succession of absentee vicars. Dr. Walsall 1591 to 1609, his namesake, Samuel Walsall 1609 to 1612 and then in 1640 Dr. Sheldon. George Bassett was the last resident vicar for many years to come. It was monstrous that successive archbishops should have abused their patronage in this way. Pluralist clergy with a number of livings or canonries lived very comfortably on the revenue of parishes, like Appledore, which they just exploited. They let the vicarage and the glebe for what they could get, and the unfortunate curate they appointed had to find his own house and feed and clothe himself and his family on the stipend he received from the absentee vicar. Whatever this was, it was less than the revenue drawn by the vicar who contributed little or nothing to the spiritual and social well being of the parish. The Archbishops of the Reformed church were no better and probably worse than the Priors of Dover in this respect.

One of the absentees, Dr. Sheldon, is of some interest. He was charged at the Archdeacon's court in 1624 for "fowlding and clathing"* his sheep in our church porch to the great offence of many people, because of the filthy stink they make". The charge went on to complain of the decay of the vicarage due to the neglect of the vicar's tenant and to the presence of hogs in the churchyard "rooting and noseling upon the graves". Dr. Sheldon admitted nothing and countercharged the churchwardens for failing to fence the church-yard, and the parish, for good measure, for providing an inadequate pulpit in the church.

Fortunately for Appledore, the curates during this shameful period of neglect by the Archbishop were men who carried out their duties with devotion, on a totally inadequate stipend.

* Clathing or clatting is the word used on Romney Marsh for the process of crutching or cutting out the clots of mucky wool between the hind legs of a sheep.

7

Many people in Appledore continued in this period to make wills, and at least 128 survive in the public records. Most of them were made by men and women with only a few personal belongings to leave, but a number dispose of the property of persons who were very comfortably off.

Three men are in this category in the last 25 years of Elizabeth I— Pascall Sloman, Henry Byam and William Lyster. All three are described as yeoman, and they clearly were affluent working farmers who lived on level terms with the local gentry in neighbouring parishes, then represented by the sons of Philip Chute. Pascall Sloman, who made his will in 1593, appointed Mr. George Chute, Esquire (*sic*) the overseer of his will and left him "a black stoned colt", Mr. Walter Chute getting an ambling bay nag. William Lyster, whose will was proved in 1599, also made George Chute, esquire, his overseer, and left him a gelding worth £10 or £10 in money. Henry Byam was perhaps rather less well off and not on quite the same social level as the other two yeomen.

Pascall Sloman had for a number of years been churchwarden, and he had married the wife of another prosperous yeoman, Thomas Ashenden. He had bought some of his father-in-law's land and owned land of his own in Wittersham. Some idea of his wealth can be got from another will—that of William Lyster, which mentions that he had entered into a bond for £2,000 to pay the legacies left by Pascall Sloman to his two nephews (he had no son). We can also get some idea of Pascall Sloman's style of farming from the stock which he left to his wife. In addition to 200 marks, her clothes, her jewels, 5 silver spoons and £20 worth of household stuff at her choice, she was given live or dead stock for the farm. This comprised 4 milch kyne, 20 ewes and 3 lambs, 1 ram, 4 seames of wheat and barley, all the hogs and poultry and 10 loads of wood. Quite a nice stock for the yeoman's widow to run the home farm.

His neighbour, William Lyster, gives less information about his property, though this was clearly substantial. He made many legacies, including £1 to each of his men and maid servants.

The entries in the transcripts of the registers of this period rarely give anything beyond the name of the person entered but, in recording the burial of William Lyster, the curate, John Hopton, wrote "a good master to the fatherless and widow".

One annoying feature of all the wills of the period is that they give little or no indication of where the testator lives. Henry Byam did his best. He left two houses in Appledore and described where they were. One of them was called "the Millhouse" and with it went "half the long entry adjoining and the herber or garden where the bees doth stand along to the well". This property is further identified as bounded "by the King's (*sic*) Street to the west and to the north and east by the testator's other house and the land of George Chowte, gent". The same "millhouse" appears in another will of 1597 when it was left by William Byam to his brother John. It would all have been clear when the bees were still there. However the King's Street is the Street. The house may have been on the east side of the Street near the site of the Swan, since in 1628 Edward Chute owned a number of fields behind the Street in this area (see map).

Rich men continued to live and work in Appledore during the seventeenth century, and in this period five parishioners qualify for this description—John Diggins, William Duplack, Robert Woolball, gent, William Easterfield and John Adams.

John Diggins (1601) left cash legacies of £250 and considerable land. William Duplack (1612) legacies of some £300. Robert Woolball (1650) some £250. These were very considerable sums of money, and in addition they had land. John Diggins' land included 30 acres at Beckard, land at "Redhill in Appledore sometimes Frenchams" and a parcel of land in Appledore itself. This is described as "between the parsonage land (on which the house now called Hallhouse Farm stands) and Chaundlers barn sometime in the occupation of Daniel Eggleden, blacksmith". William Duplack made one bequest which is of some interest, "my best horse beast to my landlord Sir Dudley Digges". Evidently he was a sub-tenant of the head tenant of the Manor Farm. Robert Woolball was a member of a well-established Appledore family of whom one was depicted at prayer in stained glass in one of the windows of the north aisle of the church (see page 25). John Adams, yeoman, was also of an established Appledore family. His land holdings extended as far as Marden, Headcorn, Wittersham and New Romney. His descendants continued to live in the parish up to the end of the nineteenth century.

These were all very comfortably well-off men. William Lyster remembered the poor of Appledore to whom he left not only 40/- a year for 5 years but a seame of wheat to be baked at his burial and given to them with cheese and beer. He was clearly a kindly man for he also left £10 to Lawrence Fann "to place him out to a tailor or otherwise".

But the most surprising example of wealth in Appledore was William Easterfield, draper, who died in 1669. His cash legacies alone amount to some £1,200, in addition to which he had considerable property in land and houses. His land included "the Red Lyon now in the occupation of George Martin". (This seems to be the first time this inn appears in the records. It was then on the opposite side of the Street—where the smithy now stands.) A tombstone was put on his grave and is now the oldest monument in the churchyard the inscription of which can still be read. "Here lyeth the body of William Easterfield of Appledore. A man worthy of his name and fortune, who departed this life the first day of June Ano Do 1669." He left ten bushels of wheat to the poor. He could have spared far more.

The other testators were men of much smaller means, but a number of them were tradesmen. They include a shoemaker (1558), a glover (1563), a tailor (1600), a chapman (1609) and a carpenter (1611). Perhaps the poorest testator of the lot was John Tuggid, the curate of Appledore from 1585 to 1594. One of his legacies was to the absentee vicar whose work he had done for nine years—"my right worshipful Mr. Doctor Walsall". He left him "my booke called the harmony upon the evangelists, if he will accept so mean a legacy".

The general impression given by these wills is that, throughout the period, the yeomen who farmed most of the land in the parish were well-to-do and lived comfortably. In addition the Street housed a number of tradesmen who, though not nearly so rich, were not too badly off. They were the lucky ones. The lot of the labourers who worked the land of the farmers was by no means so fortunate. William Easterfield is a bit of a mystery. He does not fit into the general pattern. He was a newcomer to Appledore and his wealth survived the Commonwealth, which may be of some significance.

The general layout of the village and its houses during this period is reasonably clear from documents, from the map of 1628 and from the architectural evidence of the houses which are still in the village or known to have been there in living memory. The map, unfortunately, does not show the Street southwards beyond the point where the Swan now stands, though it marks the line of the present bridle path to the Canal which then and up to 1805 was the start of the main road to New Romney along the line of the Rhee Wall. Fortunately the layout of the Street south of this point is clear from the documents. The sketch map on page 43 gives the position of the main features in this part of the Street. There was no road on the line of the modern road made in 1805, when the canal was dug, which now leads to Romney and Rye. There was, however, the broad open space which still exists, then known as the Market Place. From this led, as today, the road up the slope past Court Lodge and then down the hill towards Stone. This road led to the Ferry which had to be used to get across the Appledore Channel and so on to Stone, Wittersham and Rye (which could be reached by road only by this route). In the Market Square on the east side was the churchyard and church exactly as now. On the south side of the churchyard there were one or two houses on the site of the two houses now known as

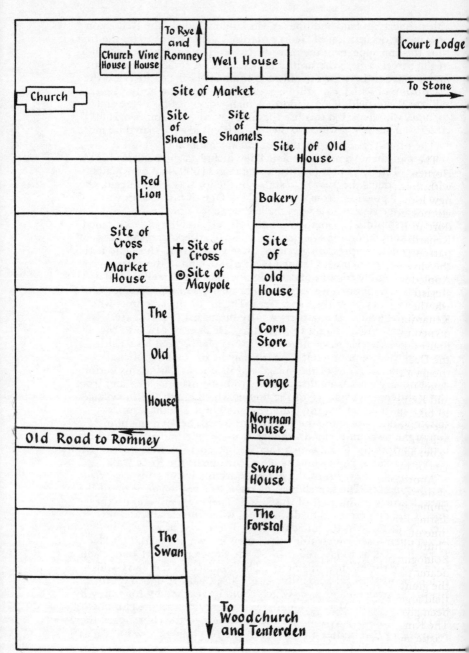

Court Lodge

To Rye and Romney

Church House | Vine House

Well House

Church

Site of Market

To Stone

Site of Shamels

Site of Shamels

Site of Old House

Red Lion

Bakery

Site of Cross or Market House

† Site of Cross

⊙ Site of Maypole

Site of old House

The

Corn Store

Old

Forge

House

Norman House

Old Road to Romney

Swan House

The Forstal

The Swan

To Woodchurch and Tenterden

Church and Vine House which incorporate part of their structure. Then came the churchyard wall. Between the churchyard and the site of the present Swan stood three houses. The first became in time the Red Lion which was pulled down by Style & Winch in the 1930s to be replaced by its present successor. Next to it was a far older building known as the Cross or Market house, pulled down in 1830. The third was the "Old House" still standing but now divided into three dwellings. By the Cross House stood the High Cross mentioned in many of the Tudor wills. At some point near this, when William Marshall, Vicar of Appledore, made his will in 1523, a maypole "had of late been sett". It is not known how long after this the maypole remained. There are no further references to it.

As you moved down the road leading to Romney you came to the Vicarage built by William Marshall in 1503. The evidence for this is a note by the Rev. John Johnson, Vicar of Appledore, 1697-1725, who said that in his time several panes of glass in the house bore William Marshall's name and this date. The house was pulled down in about 1830. It had been occupied by very few vicars. The absentee vicars let it to laymen to add to their income.

At the south end of the Market Square next to Vine House was Well house, not then separated from its neighbours by the modern road to Rye and Romney which was not built till 1805. There was however between them a drain which took the surface water from the Market Place down to the Marsh, and, probably, a footpath. On the road up the slope leading to Stone Ferry stood the Court Lodge, built between 1495 and 1517 and the oldest house in the village. Completing the square which made the market place were two houses. The most important was the complex of buildings of which the centre is now the present bakery. A sketch of this building as it was in 1799 is reproduced in Plate 4. Some of the timbers in this house are of the sixteenth and possibly the fifteenth century. The other was the adjoining house with the jetty (Swan House) which is of the same period.

In the market place itself, at the start of this period, there stood the "shamels", the booths for butchers and other traders on the pitches they rented from the manor. These occupied the whole area now grassed. As time went on the weekly markets seem to have been discontinued and trading was confined to shops, and only when the annual fair was held were the stalls set up again in the market place. All the rest of the year they were stored by the Market Beadle in the by then dilapidated Cross House, which he rented from the Dean and Chapter. Plate 3 shows the market place as it is today.

All the other houses in the Street are shown on the Cogger's map - Plate 7. Of these fifteen only five survive, Tudor Cottage and Hallhouse on the east side, Swan House, the house now called Chute House, and Bennetts on the west. On this side of the Street no houses are shown beyond Bennetts.

In the rest of the parish included in the map, only seven other

43

houses are shown. Hornes Place, with its oast houses, and Hornes Mill stand out clearly. So do a group of three houses (no longer surviving) on the crossroads of the Appledore-Woodchurch and the Stone-Warehorne road. The farmhouses of Griffin and Park Farms show up and can still be seen. The remaining house standing well back from the Woodchurch Road is possibly Oakhouse or Greenhills.

The houses shown on the map and those known to be existing at the time total thirty. This is not far short of the number of 43 householders recorded as in the parish in 1697.

The map also shows quite clearly the extent of the Hoathe or Heath. This was the waste or Common of the Manor on which all tenants had grazing or other rights. At that time it was quite a big area.

Not all the population lived in these 30 houses. Many others would have been lodged as servants or farm labourers in these houses or in the equivalent of tied cottages, small daub and wattle dwellings, of which which there are now no remains. Their occupants had little more than a bare subsistence. The entries in the Register include many entered as poor or very poor, and some of the vicars and curates not only distinguished between those who were householders and those who were not, but from time to time record a person as a "poor householder".

The statistics from the registers, analysed in Appendix IV, suggest that during this period the population was in a state of decline, and that at times disease and possibly epidemics were taking a heavy toll. In 1563 there were 37 burials and only 9 baptisms. Five years later there were 33 burials. In four years between 10 and 20 per cent of the population had died. Some better years followed, but towards the end of the sixteenth century the annual death rate was again 20 or more. The seventeenth century showed much the same experience. Two periods in particular were times of disaster. In the late 1630s the death rate was never below 20 and in 1638 reached 36. Again in 1665 the number reached 37 and in 1667 no less than 39. The Plague was of course raging in 1666 and this could have caused the heavy mortality in the last period. The end of the century showed at any rate some signs of recovery. Burials were down to single figures and the birthrate was at least showing a lead.

The numbers in the parish cannot be accurately established. The number receiving communion in 1557 is recorded as 240. In 1569 there were 60 householders and 170 communicants. In 1676 the number of inhabitants is returned as 120 excluding children, of whom only two were dissenters. In 1697 the parish returned 43 householders. The figures of householders and communicants are probably accurate enough. Entries in the register of baptisms are not necessarily a full record of all births. Burials show at least the minimum of deaths. There may have been more in times of plague when interment was hard enough to arrange and records may have slipped. With all these provisos, it is at least clear that in this period of 150 years Appledore was in decline.

8

THE 18th CENTURY

*Decay—Absentee Vicars—The gap between rich and poor—The diversion
of the Rother and the spread of ague*

This was not a happy period in Appledore's history. In the first
half of the century its population fell heavily. Christenings numbered
446, burials 538. In the second half there was some recovery.
Christenings at 578 were well ahead of burials which were down to
319. But there was probably little net increase owing to the large
number of children dying in infancy. Disease played its part. Smallpox
is recorded once, but the main killer was probably marsh fever, a.
type of malaria bred in the undrained marshes of the parish.

Appledore was not helped by having absentee vicars and absentee
landlords through this period. Three vicars spanned the whole
century, and indeed overlapped the seventeenth and nineteenth
centuries. Only one of them, John Johnson (1697 to 1725) ever lived
in the parish, and then only for four years. The other two paid
occasional visits. All three preferred to live in Cranbrook of which
they were also vicars. Appledore was far from unique in having vicars
who did little except collect part of their income from the parish for
whose spiritual welfare they were responsible. This disgraceful system
operated throughout the Church of England. In 1827 in some 10,000
parishes, only 4,400 had resident incumbents. The rest depended like
Appledore on curates appointed by the absentee incumbent for a
pitiful stipend of as little as £40 or so, whilst the incumbent drew the
balance, often a large one, of the income of the benefice.

It was bad enough when this scandalous system was operated by
lay patrons. At Appledore the patron who, throughout this century,
denied the parish a resident vicar was the Archbishop of Canterbury.
As a result, they had no less than 41 curates in a hundred years.
Many of these were most conscientious and did their best, but they
could not possibly in their short spells of office get to know their
parishioners. The parish suffered in consequence.

One of the absentee vicars, Joseph Disney (1726-1777) had in
1758 to report to the Archbishop on the state of the parish, and
there is no reason to think that the Archbishop found anything odd
in what he wrote. "I reside constantly in my vicarage house at
Cranbrook . . . 14 miles distant from Appledore. I go sometime to
Appledore. Formerly I had to go oftener but I am now advanced in
years and less able to take the journey frequently." (He was in fact
to remain Vicar for a further 20 years!) He goes on to report that he
pays his curate £40 a year and the surplice fees. He did not say that

45

out of this miserable stipend the curate had to house himself. As regards services, "There was one service each Lord's Day" at Appledore and Ebony, in the chapel then still standing on the top of Chapel Bank. "The sacrament of the Lord's Supper was administered four times a year and the number of communicants in Appledore was about twenty." Even allowing for the presence of one anabaptist and one "sottish lowbred man, John Haffenden" who never came to church, the fall in the number of communicants from the figure of 170 in 1569 and 150 in 1640 is staggering. Admittedly the reduction of the population was partly the cause. Disney returns only some 47 households against 60 in 1569, but even 47 houses should have produced more than 20 communicants. The church had reached a low ebb.

The landlords were also mainly absentees. The Dean and Chapter continued their policy of letting the most profitable part of the manor to absentees who relet it at great profit. For most of the century the tenants of Court Lodge farm were the Westrows and the Hulses, who were connected with them. The Hulses continued their tenancy till the end of the nineteenth century. Well they might. With incredible folly the Dean and Chapter allowed the lease to be drafted in such a way that in practice they could never get rid of a tenant, and they could never put up the rent. The rent remained unchanged at £59 2s. 9d. from 1600 to 1887. The Hulses, as tenants of the Dean and Chapter, were not so inhibited. They charged their sub-tenants whatever rent they could get from time to time. A valuation made in 1674 said that for many years the 740 acres were let at £900. The rent had lately been reduced and there were outgoings, particularly £60 a year for drainage rates. Even so it was a very profitable return for the Dean and Chapter's tenants, and a very unprofitable transaction for the Dean and Chapter. Appledore got no benefit and, it could be, some harm from this preposterous arrangement.

There remained some prosperous people in the parish. In this category were the Adams family, who became established in the parish in 1649, and secured the tenure of Park Hill farm. They were still there in 1833, when Thomas, a highly eccentric character, died, leaving his son Zion as the last Adams to farm Park Hill.

They had been substantial yeomen throughout this period. Thomas Adams, leaving Park Hill to his son, the last of the dynasty, in his will of 1796 described himself as "gentleman", and his will shows that in addition to Park Hill he had land in Snave, Ivychurch and Brenzett.

The Saxtons were not so prosperous, but wealthy enough to build the large house in the Street which used to bear their name, till someone decided that Saxon House was the right version. The change took place when the house was bought early in this century by a greatly respected local doctor. He thought the name, pronounced

"Sexton" was ill-omened. It also provoked another householder to produce a Norman House to balance it. William Saxton died in 1737, and in his will, in which he described himself as a grazier, he left his property to his wife, and thereafter to his daughter Ann. She married a Munk, a member of another Appledore family already on its way to prosperity. William Saxton's widow has left a letter which gives some idea of the relations between tenants in Appledore and their landlords in Canterbury, and gives a good picture of the conditions on the Marsh at the time. She evidently could not write, and whoever wrote for her was fortunately so phonetic in his spelling as to give quite a notion of how they spoke in Appledore at the time. The letter is dated May 4 day 1738, and is addressed to Mr. Samuel Norris "orrifer" living in the Great Court, Canterbury (Orrifer is perhaps how the writer pronounced "auditor"). The letter goes on:

"Sir. My service to yo and these are to bedg the faver of you to aquant the Dean an Chapter of the unfortunnot nues of the Death of my Loveing Husban William Saxton and to tell the Deene that I desinde for to leve the land which is cald the Dowles at Michelmas nix which belongs to Crist Church for the land as bin underwater ever sence Michelmas last and is likly to continue so which I shall louse the hole years Rent by it without the Dean be so good as to consider me in it so I bedg of you as soon as you have aquainted the Deene of this afear I shall be very much oblidg to yo if you will be so good as to send me a Letter by the fost post what the Deene says and whether he will be so good as to abate some of the Rent. So this from your most Humble sarvant to command.

Ann Saxton.
Her X mark."

How could the "orrifer" have resisted this moving appeal?

Two yeomen, Richard Russell (1719) and Edward Jeffery (1728) left legacies of £400 and £700 respectively, and in 1793 Mathew Palmer, bricklayer, left £400 to his daughter Anne, who thus brought some wealth to the curate, the Rev. William Jackson, whom she had married.

In a different class was Abraham Butler, Gent, who died in 1795. He left the house, known as the Huntsmans Cottage (the Roundabout House by the Warehorne Woodchurch crossroads), but this was small beer beside the legacies of £2,507 left to his relatives.

The Crosswells were also outside the ordinary run of Appledore residents. Samuel Crosswell, who died in 1742, described himself as gentleman. His son Francis, who had died before him, calls himself grocer in his will. He left everything to his father, including his stock in trade, to be invested in land for the benefit of his sister Philadelphia, the wife of Samuel Fremoult. Samuel Crosswell evidently carried out his wishes and in the process bought quite a number of houses in the Street, to add to his own property "wherein I late dwelt". This included the whole of the building (of which the bakery is now the centre) with its shop, warehouse, stable, etc., and a "spot of ground, called Pot Gally". The Pot Gally is clearly identifiable from a later plan as a triangular patch on the old road to Romney. It is now an extension of the churchyard.

Samuel left all the property to Philadelphia. Perhaps it was her idea that her father should be commemorated by the handsome large stone of black marble, weighing over a ton, now in the chancel. This has a coat of arms, which it is assumed are the arms of the Fremoult family, impaling the undoubted arms of Seager and Farewell. If so it was a filial tribute, but it was not one to which her father was entitled!

William Saxton's house had added to the houses now in the Street. About the same time the old house, now Mr. Hatch's, was built. On the same side of the Street, the Red Lion continued in business. The Queens Arms is first mentioned in the Registers in 1706. There is an Appledore tradition that it received its name because Queen Anne after coming to Appledore by water, felt thirsty and was given water from the well at Well House, then in use as an inn. It has been suggested that this Queen Anne must have been the wife of James I, because in the reign of Queen Anne it would have been impossible to have come to Appledore by water. This is certainly not so. A light draft vessel could have come up the Appledore channel much later than this period. There is moreover no mention of a Queens Arms before the eighteenth century. There is no reason to doubt the tradition, and, if it is founded on fact, the Queen who drank the Appledore water and gave her name to the inn was Queen Anne. Other inns are mentioned—the George in 1720 and the Swan in 1742. The Tithe Book of 1725 refers to a house as "lately the George Inn" so it seems to have had a rather short existence. It also refers to the Queen's Arms "when used as an inn" paying 30/-, so this inn reverted to a private house some time before this date.

A map of Kent, published in 1769, gives a surveyors impression of the houses in all the villages in the county. In Appledore it shows the eighteenth-century additions mentioned above. The Street itself remained as it was shown in the 1628 map. Those arriving from Tenterden had two choices if they were going further. They could go to Romney along the old road which turned left by the Swan to join the road on the Rhee Wall. Alternatively, when they reached the church, they could turn right and find their way to the ferry taking them to Stone and so eventually to Rye. The map shows no mills. Hornes Mill must have fallen down some time after 1628. The Manor Mill on the knoll beyond Court Lodge came down in the late eighteenth century (sometime before 1769). It was soon replaced, but not on the same spot and not in the control and monopoly of the Manor. By the end of the century corn growing was exceedingly profitable. The Corn Laws, operating in exactly the same way as the Common Agricultural Policy of the E.E.C., barred imports of foreign corn, or allowed them in only if imported at the high prices then ruling in England. By 1800 the price of wheat had risen to 26/7d. a cwt. By 1890 it was down to 7/5d. and once again the poor could afford wheaten bread. In 1790 the farmers of the district formed a cooperative and built the two mills on the Heath. They were pulled down in 1909, but until a year or so ago the octagonal base of one of these still stood. This has now been incorporated in the new house built on its foundations. This includes the stone which used to be above the doorway, inscribed "Union Mill 1791". The Mill issued tokens to those using the Mill. A sketch of the mill is reproduced in Plate 8.

But, though the farmers and some of the tradesmen thrived, the village as a whole was sunk in poverty and disease. The statistics at the start of the chapter show a population rapidly declining at the start of the century, and only just beginning to revive at the close. With the decline came poverty. The Register in 1704 refers to a parishioner "brought for burial from the new almshouse on the Heath". Later entries call it the poor house and the poor house it was. Part of this sad establishment is still standing and keeps its name of Poor Row.

Many of the burials were those of inmates of the poor house. Towards the end of the century, or possibly earlier, the overseers of the poor decided to put the relief of the poor out to contract. Thomas Adams, of Park Hill Farm, the last of the family, took on this office. He was a thorn in the flesh of the curates. He professed great admiration for the doctrines of the French Revolution, and buried his children, and himself was buried, in a brick vault which he built in a field next to his house. Whether his Republican and anti-clerical principles made him a humane pauper farmer cannot be established. All through this unhappy century the inhumane working of the poor law can be seen in operation. The curates carefully enquired and recorded the parish of origin of any strangers or newcomers. They noted whether they had a certificate—the document secured whenever possible by a person leaving his own village to seek work elsewhere. This certificate enabled him to claim poor relief from the parish he had left. It also enabled any parish to which he had migrated to refuse him poor relief and to return him to his village of origin.

Just because it was so important to ensure the right to poor relief in hard times, parents took good care to have their children's birth recorded in the register. In 1792 Robert Beane (almost certainly one of the old Appledore family of Beane or Beaney) had an affidavit sewn into the register to record the christening of his son John at Appledore which had been left out "by some ommission".

Even more remarkable were the entries for several years of the births of the children of Richard Russell. The entry always takes the same form, e.g.: Stephen Russell, born 10th March 1715, an unbaptised infant is desired to be registered here". That secured the infant Russell the right to parish relief if in later life he needed it. But he was not baptised for reasons which emerge in a later entry of May 1721. Five unbaptised Russell children then received baptism "the parents of the above children adhered for some time to a certain sect called Seekers—a sort of Mungrel Independents. Richard, the father, during his lifetime, would never consent to have them baptised, and after his decease the widow was with great difficulty prevailed upon to let them be baptised. N.B. Russell, whose father was a Quaker, was a disciple of one Skeats of Tenterden". It must have been a great humiliation for Richard Russell to have to enter his children's birth in the register of a church for which he had no use. He could not, however, afford to take the risk of depriving them of the right to relief. The fear of "pauperism", and the even greater fear of not having even the last resort of parish relief, was ever present in the minds of those who, at best, could only look forward to bare subsistence.

The underpaid curates did their best for their poor and disease ridden parishioners. Some of them showed almost excessive devotion in ensuring baptism for the sickly infants who arrived so frequently. Time and again the registers record baptisms administered in the home with a note "periclitans" = in danger, or "in articulo mortis"— on the point of death. Sometimes the child was later brought to church to be received into the congregation. All too often death followed in a matter of hours or days. This zeal should not be mocked. The curates considered it their duty, and they ran considerable risk in entering houses where fever was raging. They knew the conditions under which the people were living. They also knew at firsthand how difficult it was to make both ends meet. Less commendable was the zeal of other curates in insisting on public penance by those who had anticipated the marriage ceremony. In 1725, Thomas Johnson and Thomas Sharp brought the children of their marriages for christening five weeks after their marriage. This was too much for the curate and they and their wives had to do public penance in the church. Appledore was not alone in continuing this old practice. Indeed as late as 1849 penance was enforced at a village near Cambridge for another offence, that of defamation. In this village the village fiddler applied a very rude word to the Rector's wife. He was brought to church to do penance, but the only result was catcalls, a shower of hassocks, riot, and the fiddler carried off for drinks at the pub.

In general the curates did their best, for a miserable salary in a climate which did no good to their health, in ministering to a parish afflicted with disease and poverty. In entering in the register the ugly word "pauper" or even "native pauper" they were recording for posterity the affliction of their flock. They may not have known it but when they wrote "native" they were using the same word as their medieval predecessors had when describing the children of the serfs of the manor. The poor of Appledore at this time were little better off.

Not all the curates were so conscientious and so acutely aware of the appalling conditions in which most of their parishioners lived. In Appendix VI is a letter written in the spring of 1781 by the Rev. William Jackson. He had come to Appledore as its curate in December 1779 and was lodging in a set of rooms in the old vicarage built by William Marshall round about 1500. He evidently thought it the height of comfort, though in 1815 the Vestry considered it a slum and a disgrace to the village and petitioned for its demolition—a fate which it suffered a few years later.

In his bachelor chambers he could not avoid the stink of the marshes or the knowledge that the marsh was the source of the ague that afflicted so many of his 'parasioners', and might infect him at any time. He gazed through rose tinted spectacles at the ships sailing from Rye to London—salt water still flowed at high tide up the channel from Rye to Appledore and there were no trees or road to block the view. With the same rosy vision presumably he looked on his parishioners at large. In his letter he mentions only the eligible young ladies who came to take tea with him in his rooms; one of them he was to marry very shortly. They were the daughters of the rich graziers in Appledore and it was with them in mind that he wrote 'people here are very wealthy and live on the fat of the land'.

His letter, then, gives a misleading picture of the life of most of the people who had to support a family on 8s. a week. It is far better as a contemporary account of what the village looked and smelt like and of how the well-to-do lived.

A truer picture of how the greater part of the people fared is given by Hasted. Writing in 1798 he says of the village: 'It contains 48 houses and 320 inhabitants. The village is situated very low, close to the marshes . . . the houses are but meanly built and most inhabited by graziers, lookers* and smugglers. The vast quantity of marshes which lie contiguous and come close to it, make it very unhealthy, and this is rendered much more so by a large tract of swamp called the Dowles . . . the large quantity of stagnating water continually on these engenders such noxious and pestilential vapours as spread sickness and frequent death on the inhabitants . . . the sickly countenances of them plainly discovering the unwholesome air they breathe in." That must have been a fair reflection on what life was like in Appledore at the end of the eighteenth century, except for its better off parishioners. houses and 320inhabitants.

The smell of decay from the marshes and the ague, a form of malaria, spread by the mosquitoes which flourished in the stagnant waters, was caused by bad drainage. The Appledore channel had provided a reasonable, if not fully adequate, outfall for the tidal waters—for many centuries, so long as it was the main outlet for the

* Sheep and cattle minders.

51

Rother and a seaway on which ships could sail. Unfortunately for Appledore, the landlords up river were allowed during the early 18th century to dig a channel which diverted the river to its present course to the west of the Isle of Oxney. Appledore ceased to be a port, but the tide continued to flow up to Smallhythe and to ebb, ever more sluggishly down to the sea at Rye. That was the cause of the stagnant marshes, of the ague and of the 'sickly countenances' of the inhabitants. The remedy was not to come till the Royal Military Canal was dug in 1805.

THE ROYAL MILITARY CANAL
The scare of Invasion by Napoleon

The construction of the Royal Military Canal between 1804 and
1807 was of such importance to Appledore that it needs a chapter to
itself. The canal was designed to save the country from invasion by
Napoleon. It never had to stand the test and critics have mocked it as
a military folly. They were probably wrong, but even if they were
right, the canal stands justified. Thanks to it, the Dowles and the
other swamps round Appledore were drained. Marsh fever was
eventually driven out and Appledore became a healthy place. The
population increased after many years of decline, and the foundations
were laid for a happier future.

The Royal Navy had for many years been masters of the narrow
seas but, as long as they depended, as they did, on sail, they could
not guarantee the country's immunity against landings on the coast
of Kent. The narrow straits between England and France could
always be crossed by a strong continental power whenever the winds
held the Navy down Channel.

Invasion was never, until the war of 1939-45, more imminent
than in the war with France, which started in 1793 and ended only
after Waterloo in 1815. As early as 1794 the risk was considered
serious enough to require plans for evacuating the cattle off the
Marsh into the greater safety of the Weald. As part of the plan, all
carts and wagons in Appledore and the neighbouring villages were
listed and numbered. It may be that they were intended to remove
the inhabitants to safety, along with the livestock. Twenty-one
farmers in Appledore were appointed drovers, under the direction of
two "conductors" and one "Chief Conductor". Amongst them are
the familiar names of Bates, Boon and Strickland all of whom have
descendants still living in the parish. The plan had just about as much
chance of success as the similar plan in 1914. The carts, the drovers
and the flocks and herds were to proceed down the Street to Moor
Lane and from thence to what is now St Michael's Tenterden, and
eventually to Cranbrook. Why they were not to go by the Reading
Street road is not explained. Perhaps that was to be kept clear for the
military. The existence of this plan shows how seriously the Government was taking the threat of invasion even before Napoleon had
become the terror of Europe.

The threat was far graver in 1803 when the short-lived peace of
1801 came to an end. British intelligence was good (greatly helped by

valuable information from defectors). It was known that Napoleon was building a large invasion fleet of landing craft in the Pas de Calais, and that his plans provided for them to make their beach head east or west of Dungeness, on whichever side of the headland the wind required. The Army staff also had a plan—to confine Napoleon in his beach head by the simple device of flooding Romney Marsh. The Dutch had kept out invaders in just this way and it was assumed that all that was needed was to open the sluices in the sea wall and let the sea surge in to cover the marsh beneath the waters of the channel.

Fortunately we had a good general—General Sir David Dundas, who started life in the army as a private and ended as a Field Marshal. He in turn had a first rate staff officer in Lt.-Colonel John Brown, who was responsible for field works. Early in 1804 Brown had worked out that it would need three or four tides to flood even part of the marshes. A little later he discovered that only at the high tides would the sea effectively flood the marsh at all. In short the staff plan on which the whole defence scheme hinged was based on false assumptions and would not work. Even before the second fallacy in the plan had been discovered, Colonel Brown had proposed the canal as an alternative scheme of containing the invasion. At that stage he was thinking of a canal covering the 19 miles from Shorncliffe to Rye. Later it was decided to extend it from Rye to Fairlight.

The object of the new plan was to narrow the front to be defended from 30 miles of coast to 19 miles of canal. The canal would not only be a line—admittedly a very narrow line—of defence, but it would provide means of bringing up reinforcements to the threatened points, moving either by barge or on the road to be made on the defender's side of the canal. This would be screened from enemy fire throughout its length by the parapet built with the soil thrown up by the navvies digging the canal. Napoleon's invading armies would first have to face the shore batteries in the Martello towers on the coast. They would then have to cross the marsh, not flooded but criss-crossed by innumerable dykes. All the time (admittedly unless there was fog) they would be in full view from the high ground under which the canal flowed. If they advanced in fog they would probably get lost anyway. From the heights the artillery would bombard the advancing parties and infantry would enfilade any enemy troops attempting to cross the reaches of the canal, laid out in echelon for this purpose.

The scheme was not as silly as armchair critics like Barham in the Ingoldsby Legends or Cobbett in his Rural Rides made out. It could have worked. It could at least have held the invasion for long enough to allow the Royal Navy a chance to destroy the landing craft on which the French would have had to rely for supplies.

Anyhow the plan was considered good enough to be immediately approved by Pitt in September 1804. Work began in November. The sector to Rye was finished in time for a formal opening in 1806, by the Commander in Chief, the Duke of York, who was a valuable and energetic supporter of the scheme throughout. It could have been serviceable for defence some months earlier.

The job had been done at great speed, and at a cost which now seems fantastically low: £140,870 19s. 10½d.—against an estimate of £200,000.

A canal thirty feet wide and seven feet deep had been driven from Shorncliffe to Fairlight. The extension over the last sector was not finished till 1807. The men who did the job had no mechanical excavators. They dug two cubic yards a day with nothing but their own muscle power. Their only mechanical aid was a steam pump used when the diggings flooded. The work was started by 360 labourers and 600 navigators (as the professional canal diggers were then called). These were employed by contractors, who were under the direction of Rennie, the celebrated Civil Engineer. After a time the contractors went bankrupt. Rennie gave up his post. Brown then finished the job with some 500 labourers and three regiments of militia reinforced by detachments of the Royal Staff Corps and the Royal Wagon Train, the predecessors of the Royal Engineers and the Royal Army Service Corps.

It had been an achievement, and, even if its effectiveness was not tested, the money spent on the canal was not wasted. Even when he first formulated his plan, Brown had pointed out that the canal could have commercial use. So, in fact, it did. For a number of years a regular barge service was maintained between Hythe and Rye, and the building now occupied by Messrs Haynes at Appledore bridge housed the barge horses owned by Nathan Bates of the well-known Appledore family, who in later times have adapted themselves to other means of transport.

The Government gradually lost their interest in the canal as a defence work. The Royal Staff Corps, whose men had maintained the canal up to then, was disbanded in 1829. One of their number, James Wyatt, who had been present at Waterloo (as had one of the farmers, Daniel Ayer, selected for the evacuation team of 1793) decided to settle in Appledore. Here he followed his old army trade of bricklayer, and here he was buried. His tombstone, displaced to make way for a later memorial, has been rescued and is now in a place of honour in the church.

The Government did not finally abandon the canal till 1877, when they let the bed of the canal for 999 years to the Lords of the Level of Romney Marsh, then the drainage authority for the Marsh. Their successors in title—the Kent River Authority, destined to become the Southern Water Authority, still hold the lease and are responsible for its upkeep and use. The canal bank on the parapet side was not sold by the War Office until 1935, when it was finally decided that it had no use for defence. A few years later they had to requisition it again, since, after all, it still was needed for its original purpose. It was refortified as one of the lines of defence against the Nazi invaders. They, like Napoleon, failed to cross it.

In the 1935 sale Miss Dorothy Johnston, who had lived for many years in Appledore, bought the sector between Appledore and Warehorne bridges. She immediately presented it to the National Trust, together with an endowment for its upkeep.

The commercial use of the canal had petered out by the middle of the nineteenth century. The building of the railway from Ashford to Hastings in 1851 took away any profitability it still had. But it had by then saved Appledore from decay.

Up to the building of the canal Appledore had been cut off effectively from Rye. In earlier years you could get to Rye by sea down the Appledore channel. By then the channel was nearly silted up and was little more than a nuisance stopping any direct road to Rye, and flooding the marshes which lay between. The construction of the canal turned the channel into a blind ditch. In its place for many years Appledore enjoyed a regular barge service between Hythe and Rye. They also got a road. It was an essential part of the defence plan that behind the parapet, throughout its length, there should be a road along which troops could march to man whichever sector was under attack. This road was metalled throughout its length by beach (pebbles brought up from Hythe by barge). For the greater part of its length the grass now grows over the road, though you can easily find it with a spade. Between Appledore and Rye the modern road has the old beach road as its bottom foundation. Up to 1917 little seems to have been done to improve the original surface. A. G. Bradley, when he bicycled from Appledore to Rye in that year complained that it was "gravelly, well enough for heavy lorries or even cars, but for a cycle of any kind it is to be avoided"! Whatever its short-comings the new road, crossing the canal by its bridge, was now connected with the Street, and Appledore had a direct road link with Rye. It became far less isolated, and with its road and canal links was back again nearer to the palmier days of the past when it had been a sea port.

At first the canal must have been an eyesore, with its parapet breaking the contours between marsh and upland throughout its long length. Oddly enough, although still required as a defence work, it was planted with trees as early as 1807. Elms and thorn were both planted, and planting continued as late as the twenties. The two Relf brothers of Appledore, one of whom, Edward Relf, lived in Bennets and did not die till he was 101, claimed to have planted all of them. There may be some exaggeration in this but they certainly planted a great number in the Appledore sector. They make the canal bank a lovely sight. Nearly all the elms planted were of the broad leaved Huntingdon variety which resists Dutch Elm disease as well as any. Even they have suffered and the canal has lost nearly all its elms. Other trees have been planted.

56

The most important by-product of the Military Canal from the point of view of Appledore was neither its beauty nor even the opening up of communications. The most valuable benefit it conferred was in quite another field. Most of Romney and a large part of Walland Marsh was by this time well drained. Appledore still had noisome marshes in the Dowles and along the course of the Appledore channel from Appledore to Ebony and Smallhythe. This not only reduced the profitability of the land. It was the source of the marsh fever which had such disastrous effects on the health of the parish. All the improvements did not come at once. Pumping stations were needed and in time these were provided, but much of the operation depended for its success on the existence of the canal as a regulator of the water level in the low land on both its banks. Today it is almost impossible to imagine the well-drained fertile land, a lot of it under the plough, which now extends over all the low lying areas between Appledore and the hills behind, as at best rough grazing and at worst saltings and swamp. This miracle owes much to the Canal.

10

POVERTY AND DESPAIR IN THE 19th CENTURY

One unhappy feature of the first half of the nineteenth century was the distressing and alarming spread of poverty. Appledore's experience, though typical, was no worse than that of nearly all other villages. Both in the countryside and in the new industrial towns the rapidly rising cost of food brought grinding poverty and misery. This and the stubborn refusal to raise wages in line with the cost of bread was the cause of the great misery which culminated in the last labourer's revolt in 1830.

In country parishes, on the face of it, this should have been a time of prosperity, not of disaster. Farming, the source of nearly all the countryside's wealth, had never had it so good. The price of corn rose to phenomenal heights. Wheat had averaged a fairly steady 7/6d. a cwt. from 1700 to 1775. Prices then started to rise and spiralled rapidly. Between 1800 and 1820 wheat sold at an average at 20/-. In 1812 it reached 29/6d. These, from the farmer's point of view, were staggeringly good prices which were remembered sadly in the 1890s, when the price was 5/-, the price to which wheat fell again in the 1930s. The farmers and owners of land and tithe became exceedingly rich.

The farmers did not share any of their new riches with their labourers. Throughout this unhappy period all the land interests were obsessed with the idea that, once they started putting up the labourer's wages, ruin was inevitable. Corn prices could fall but, if the wage had once been raised, they would never be able to get it down again.

So they kept the labourer's wage at 7/- a week, whilst the price of wheat trebled, and in the worst years quadrupled. Wheaten bread was the labourer's staple food washed down with tea flavoured with sugar. He could not afford milk . He just could not live on his wage and the parish had to relieve his distress out of the poor rate.

The parish had had this duty ever since the Poor Laws of Queen Elizabeth had been passed. The poor rate was assessed at so many pence in the pound on the rent of all property. The rate was fixed by the Vestry (an institution to which all ratepayers belonged) and relief was administered by Overseers appointed by it. In these bad times the Vestries and their overseers did their best to help their poor neighbours, but their efforts were marred by one appalling error of policy. This was the practice, known as the Speenhamland system after the district which was one of the first to adopt it, of granting relief in the form of a supplement to the inadequate wage paid by the farmer. Its most disastrous consequence was to remove any chance of the farmers ever increasing wages to an adequate level, reflecting their own prosperity and the greatly increased cost of food on which it was founded. Until a more adequate wage was eventually paid, pauperism was a harsh feature of village life. It was only to be brought within more reasonable limits when agricultural wages started to increase over the second half of the century. Even this improvement was to be checked by the great agricultural depression of the 80s. This started when the prairies of America and of Australia opened up, and their corn, grown at a much lower cost, came flooding in. Thanks to the repeal of the corn laws this far cheaper corn was no longer kept out but brought the price of bread down with a run. This was disaster for the farmer, but the salvation of the labourer and his family, despite the reduction in their wages.

Some impression of Appledore's experience in this period can be gained from the Vestry records, which survive for most of the relevant period from 1792 to 1834. It is a sombre picture of honest men reduced to pauperism and driven to despair.

The growing poverty can be gauged by the amount spent on relief, and the occasional records of the number of "pauper" families. In 1792 the sum spent from the Poor Rate was £302. By 1818 this had risen to £972, the produce of a rate of 2/9d. In addition, in most of the latter years, a highway rate of 1/- in the pound was also levied. Since most of this fund was spent on wages to out-of-work labourers set to work on the roads, the figure of £972 was supplemented from this source by up to a further £250.

This expenditure on relief at the rate of £100 a month is in accord with the number of pauper families recorded. In 1819, for example, there were 27 families, including 75 children. With the parents included, the number of paupers comes to some 120. The census returns show that the population of Appledore reached 560 in 1821 and stayed at this level in 1831 and 1841. One person in five was a pauper. It was worse still in 1833—182 persons in a population of 560—so that one in three were paupers. These families were not just vagrants or casual workers. Most of them were householders who normally would have been paying (admittedly a very small) tax towards the parish poor rate. In 1838, when they had become recipients of relief, 25 such families had formally to be excused payment of poor rate.

These records prove clearly that poverty spread fast and wide through Appledore.

The real remedy undoubtedly was to increase agricultural wages but even if this had been done there would still have been some unemployment in the parish. Yet the system made it appallingly difficult to seek work in another village or in a town. It was a fundamental principle of the Poor Law system that a parish's obligation was limited to looking after its own poor. For this reason far too much time (and money) was spent by the Overseers in removing strangers arriving in the parish and those not technically entitled to a settlement. In theory the pass system should have dealt with the problem of seeking work outside the village. The overseers could issue a pass to a parishioner wishing to remove to another parish. This certified that he had a "settlement" in Appledore and that if he became destitute in another village, Appledore would pay for his relief and his return. However, it was not, in practice, easy to get passes, though the Appledore accounts show how the system worked. Temporary relief was given to passholders and all travellers "in distress" got a dole of 6d. or 1/- before being sent on their way. If, however, an Appledore family became a longer charge on the poor rate of another parish, the overseers had to bring them back to get their relief in Appledore. In general, moreover, the prospect of getting work in another parish was remote. Inside the parish, if you were lucky enough to be in work, your fate was almost inevitably to be supported out of the poor rate to supplement a wage which could not feed, house and clothe your family.

Given the limits within which they had to work, the Vestry and the overseers did all they could to treat their neighbours humanely. Their policy changed from time to time but a number of their decisions were wise and compassionate.

The worst of all fates for a pauper was the workhouse. Even in living memory the workhouse was a place of despair, little better than a prison. At the start of this period, parishes could, if they wished, form unions of three or four parishes to build and run a workhouse. Between 1792 and 1834 Appledore subscribed in turn to the workhouse at Willesborough, at Brookland, at Hamstreet and at Tenterden. It seems, however, that they sent parishioners to these houses of despair with reluctance and only as a last resort. The first entry is in 1795 when four paupers were carried to Willesborough by the overseers, and £14 a quarter was paid for their maintenance. By 1797 the number had risen to five. In 1800 a child was sent there, a terrible thing to happen. By 1812 Brookland workhouse was being used. £133 was paid out in that year, a high proportion of the poor relief of £871. In 1807 something unrecorded happened to cause the Vestry to decide that Brookland should be entirely relinquished and the children there taken away. Indeed until 1823 there is no further mention of sending parishioners to a workhouse. In that year the Vestry agreed to take up to six places at Brookland, but it is doubtful whether this idea was pursued. In 1832 an agreement was made with Hamstreet workhouse. This could hold 40 and Appledore's quota was 10. Two years later the Poor Law Act of 1834 made drastic alterations in the Poor Law system. The Vestry lost almost all its powers to relieve distress. The task devolved on the newly established Guardians and the larger Unions to which parishes were compulsorily assigned. From now on the parish records cease and the poor of Appledore were at the mercy of the Tenterden Union.

The above records support the theory that in Appledore the Vestry avoided the workhouse whenever possible. The cynical may say that this was an expensive form of relief, but there is further evidence to suggest a more humane motive. There is a tradition that Thomas Adams, the tenant of Park Hill farm, and a man of liberal, even revolutionary ideas, "farmed the poor", and there are large payments to him in 1818 and 1819. It is possible that he contracted to maintain poor persons who would otherwise have been sent to the workhouse, and that his motives in taking on the task were not wholly mercenary. Again in 1822, shortly before he died, the Vestry rented some 12 houses in the parish for the use of the poor. This could have been done to prevent recourse to the workhouse.

The village in any case had one safeguard against the workhouse. About 1700 what the Parish Register refers to as the new Almshouses on the Heath were built. These were on the site of the two houses still known as Poor House Row. In 1800 we know from a casual entry of "one guinea paid to the Militia from Reading Barracks attending to the Fire of the Poor House" that Poor Row was badly damaged. We also know from a payment of £200 the following year that a new poor house on the same site was built. In its old and new form this range of five small dwellings was the first refuge of the poor. They paid 1/6d. a week and had the use of the garden in front of the house. It must have been a great boon in those days. It was not till 1872 that the Poor Houses on the 1½ acres of land were finally sold to Henry Green for £255 and the proceeds used to extend the present village school. In their last years they had not been fully occupied, which suggests that the worst of the poverty was by then over.

Another admirable feature of the overseers' policy was whenever possible to provide work. Work on the roads, paid for out of the highway rate, has already been mentioned. There was another quite elaborate scheme for farm work evolved in 1830. All farmers were given a quota of 2 men for each acre of arable and 1 man for each acre of pasture. Each farmer taking up his quota got 1/- a day for a married man and 2d. for a single man. Any labourers who did not receive this employment were "surplus" and eligible for outdoor relief. This was Speenhamland at its worst but with the mitigating feature of inducing farmers to employ as many men as possible.

A sad practice was putting children out to board. Grants were paid to those who took them (usually at the rate of 3/6d. a week). In 1832, for example, there were 25 children out at board. In some cases, where the mother had died, this system was almost inevitable, and at least, in most cases the children were in the same parish as their family. Others, less lucky, were sent as far away as Bethersden and Hythe. These

61

children and some adults also got clothing grants. These were set out in full detail (nearly always including "scuffles" or "scuffling aprons" for those working in the fields) and the all male Vestry decided which articles were necessary and which articles were just women's frippery. "Stays" were almost always refused on principle, although stuff for stays got through.

Other benefits were given in kind. Faggots were issued once a year to all on the list and, most valuable of all, issues of flour were made. With wheat at 30/- a cwt. this was the most helpful means of shielding the poor from the effects of a rise in the cost of food.

Just as beneficial was a free medical service. Mr. Bignall, the Appledore doctor, was paid a fee, which started at 25 guineas in 1819 and was up to £40 in 1823, for which he attended on all the poor in Appledore. In 1819 he was paid 3/- a head for inoculating poor persons against "the small or cow pox". Before this system had started there had been occasional special payments for medicine—"a bottle of British Balsam" for Dame Terry in 1793 cost 1/-. In 1801 4/- was paid for Bark (i.e. quinine) for Mr. Goldsmith's ague—a reminder of the prevalence of marsh fever at that time.

Appledore's private National Health Service, run by Dr. Bignall, must have been effective. In many of the large poor families the children's ages are recorded, and up to ten are shown in a single family so that infant mortality was evidently very low.

Finally there is evidence of consideration and kindness. In 1799 Mrs. Bailey was buried by the parish. This they had to do. What they did, without any obligation, was to pay a neighbour for sitting up with her in her last hours, laying her out and finding a home for her three children (who were looked after at the cost of the parish for many years after).

All this was on the credit side, and the overseers may also claim some credit for the fact that Appledore took no part in the Labourer's Revolt in 1830. The nearest incident on record is at Ruckinge, and either the labourers at Appledore were too broken to join the movement, or they felt that the farmers of the parish were doing their best for them.

Also on the credit side was the help which the parish gave to those in Appledore who could see no future for their families in the village and wished to emigrate. In the 20s and 30s some 30 persons emigrated to the U.S.A., Canada and Australia, with the help of the passage money from the Vestry. An entry in 1834 shows that Rye was a port from which emigrant ships then sailed. In that year Mr. and Mrs. George Bourne decided to emigrate to the U.S.A., and applied for £18. The Vestry agreed to enquire for any sailings from Rye and the price. In the 1850s about the same number also decided to try for a better life in the New World.

These were bad times, and the tolerance of the totally unnecessary poverty when agriculture was flourishing was a disgrace to the whole country. The Appledore Vestry and the overseers were humane men, and Jacob Kingsnorth, for many years the chairman, was an exceptionally kind hearted man, but the system they had to administer provided no cure for poverty and was humiliating to those who had to "live on the parish". They had to ask for relief in person. Those who got it had their names posted on the church door. Those who refused to attend the Vestry got no relief. Relief was subject to a means test. No relief was paid till all savings and resources had been exhausted. Occasionally even the formal records of the Vestry show the effect on the applicants of having to justify their requests for relief. In 1817 Solomon Giles asked the Vestry to pay his rent. The Chairman said on behalf of the Meeting "We cannot think of paying your rent under all circumstances considered. In reply to which Master Giles said I can not go on any longer, nor won't try".

There is no reason to doubt that these were the authentic words spoken in despair by one of those who suffered in these dark days of poverty in the midst of plenty in the countryside.

11

NINETEENTH-CENTURY FARMERS AND LANDOWNERS
The Chute Estate and the Manor fade out.

Not everyone in Appledore was living on a bare subsistence. That was the fate of the majority—the labourers and their families. Others were comfortably off, and some were very rich.

The richest group were the farmers and, of the farmers, by a long way the richest were the Munks. The family had arrived in Appledore in the seventeenth century. The founder of their fortunes was William Munk who fathered six sons and four daughters between 1701 and 1722. Four of them were endowed with a strong urge and capacity to make money and climb the social scale. William, the eldest, was born at Park Farm in 1701 and lived there till his death in 1776. This he liked to be known as the Great House on the Heath—a typical Munk gesture. He married Elizabeth, the daughter and heiress of William and Ann Saxton, thus securing eventually for the Munks both Saxton and Well House. It was their second son, Jeffery, who first set the pace for the family. He got a lease of the old Horne estate in Kenardington and made a small fortune. He was able to live as one of the gentry, first at Little Hornes in Kenardington and later (1817) in Saxton House. He kept a pack of hounds. He had a family vault built for him in the South Chapel, where his mason swept aside the remains of Philip Chute to make way for the new gentry. Here he was buried in 1817, leaving amongst other possessions 4,000 ewes and 400 oxen, a fair record of his place in the grazier's league. Thomas Paine, a cordwainer or bootmaker, married his daughter. Their son, another Thomas Paine, succeeded to much of his grandfather's fortune. He used part of it in 1840 to pull down the old Forstal, another Munk house, and to build the present house with its elegant facade. He also built the elaborate tomb in the churchyard which commemorates him as Thomas Paine, gentleman.

Another Jeffery Munk, cousin of the Master of Hounds, had done just as well as a farmer and grazier. His only misfortune was his son-in-law, a man called Wilkinson. He induced his father-in-law to back his speculations in corn—in which great fortunes could, at that time, be made and lost. He lost, fled the country and left his wife without support and his father-in-law to deal with the creditors. Jeffery Munk went bankrupt, and had to sell his house, the old Forstal, and all his other property. His holdings on Shirley Moor alone fetched £4,450. His son George was glad enough to marry Ann Saunders, daughter of the landlord of the Swan, which he kept after his father-in-law retired to the house he had built across the Street, known for many years as Saunders and now as Pindrop Cottage.

Another of old William Munk's four sons, John Munk, had, many years before, got the lease of Court Lodge from the Hulses. When he died in 1795, the residue alone of his great estate came to £9,000. It was his grandson, George Munk, who reached the highest point of the family's fortunes, only to end in total failure. He too lived in Court Lodge and held the lease of the farm. Nearly all the Munks were shrewd judges of sheep and cattle, of great skill in farm management, and keen men of business. When corn prices rose they were equally successful with their arable farming. (Even in 1841 there were 534 acres under the plough, in the parish, in addition to the 2,070 acres of pasture.) George Munk secured a countrywide reputation. It was a time when the aristocracy were taking a leading part in improving the breeding of farmstock and farming methods generally. The Dukes of Bedford and Norfolk among others sat at the feet of George Munk. The Duke of Bedford passed what must have been for him three rather uncomfortable nights in Court Lodge in order to see George Munk's stock and to learn something of his system of management. General Sir Samuel Hulse, basking in the glory reflected from his famous sub-tenant, got his friend the Prince Regent to get a lucrative appointment for him, supplying fodder for the cavalry regiments in Kent and Sussex. This was the summit of the Munk fortunes. They had not only great wealth but they were hob-nobbing with the greatest in the land.

The pace could not last. George Munk began to neglect his sheep, his property and his business. His debts piled up. His marriage to his cousin Rebecca—a shotgun wedding with the gun held by their common grandfather—had not been a success and they had separated. It was his wife, so it was said, who instituted bankruptcy proceedings, and by 1815 George Munk was bankrupt. He lived on till 1864, a sad old man, lodging with Thomas Avery, one of his farm labourers and father of Edward Avery the village grocer and postmaster. Jacob Kingsnorth was the only mourner who followed him to his grave.

While their fortune lasted, the Munks ruled the village. In 1800 the rateable value of the land owned or occupied by seven members of the family was £1,187. That left only £2,285 for the rest of the parish. In the vestry the number of votes a ratepayer had increased with the value of his property. If they wanted to, the Munks could carry any proposal. If need be they could bring in the votes of the Stricklands with whom they were connected by marriage. The Strickland's land was rated at £482 and they alone could talk on level terms with the Munks. They may also have had the same social aspirations. In 1809 Edmund Strickland wrote to the Dean and Chapter asking for leave to hunt and shoot over the manor "for we are raising a pack of dogs in the parish".

The Munk empire had almost totally collapsed by 1840. In that year tithes, hitherto paid in kind (the tenth sheaf, the tenth lamb, etc.), was commuted for annual cash payments. Appledore, like all other parishes, was assessed after a complete survey showing all the occupiers and owners of land in the parish. According to this document there were then four large farmers in the parish. William Cock had Court Lodge Farm (380 acres), Howard Smith farmed Gusborne, Greenfield and the Dowles (260 acres). The Adams at Park Hill and Hornbrook and Thomas Walker at Park Farm had some 230 acres apiece. The Kingsnorths at Gusborne had 100 acres but the Stricklands had lost nearly all their land. Only one Munk remained on the list with 100 acres on Shirley Moor. There still remained 50 acres on the Heath. There had been almost a total turnover of farmers in the parish, and the Munks who had ruled over all had virtually vanished from sight.

There were to be more changes as the lean years of the nineteenth century closed in. The great prairies of the New World were about to flood the market with cheap corn, to the great benefit of the nation but to as great a loss to the farmers. The graziers were also to see the discovery of refrigeration and the arrival of Canterbury lamb from New Zealand, beef from the Argentine and wool from the Southern hemisphere. Farms changed hands again. There always seemed to be one man who weathered the storm, often, but not always, the tenant of Court Lodge Farm. There was also scope for the smaller farmer better able to tighten his belt and wait, or let his descendants wait, for better times. In 1841 Joseph Pearson had no more than 28 acres. By the beginning of the next century Thomas Joseph Pearson was to be the biggest farmer in the parish. For many farmers, however, the struggle was too great. It was their turn to suffer the disasters that had fallen on their labourers a hundred years before.

The fortunes of landowners waxed and waned with those of their tenants. There was less change at first, but in the course of the century all the traditional landowners were to disappear. The Manor of Canterbury had been a great stabilising influence. In law they owned the freehold of every acre in the parish. In practice, moreover, their policy, ever since Tudor times, of letting the farmland in large blocks to rich families, resulted in most of the land remaining in the same ownership for many generations, and in some cases for centuries. These tenants of the manor were in fact, though not in theory, the effective landowners. They could sell their leases but they had little incentive to do so. The rent they paid the manor was low. The rent they charged their farm tenants gave them a fair return even when farming was in the doldrums.

The most stable of all the tenancies was that of Court Lodge (which accounted for a quarter of all the land in the parish). The Hulse family held this on lease from the manor for nearly three centuries. Their tenure was to be broken only when the Ecclesiastical Commissioners in 1888 took over the landed estates of Canterbury Cathedral. They had been given these powers earlier in the century to provide better management for Cathedral and other church property which had been grossly mismanaged. The Commissioners paid the Hulses £14,000 to surrender their, in practice, perpetual lease. It was good business. The manor had received a rent which had never been raised from the sum of £59 2s. 9d. fixed in Tudor times. From now on the Commissioners would get the current rent paid by the tenant. Since it was the best land in the parish, the rent was a high one. The Court Lodge, still incorporating the remnants of the house built between 1495 and 1517, but with many later additions, had been largely pulled down in 1873, and completely in 1885. A sketch of the old Lodge is reproduced in Plate 9. The Ecclesiastical Commissioners built the present house on the same site in their inimitable style of architecture. In time—as it turned out at the wrong time—the Commissioners sold the property and it came into private ownership. It is now owned by the Crown Commission.

The other large landowners had been the Chutes, who held, under lease from the manor, almost as much land as the Hulses (see the 1628 map). The Chutes of Bethersden came to an end in the eighteenth century. Their property passed in 1721 to the Austens of Tenterden (soon to become Baronets) and, when their line died out, came to the niece of Sir Edward Austen's widow, the wife of Mrs. Liberty Taylor of Maidstone. The Taylors petered out and, on the death in 1882 of old Miss Taylor, the estate was broken up after over three hundred years. The farms were for most part bought by the tenants. An estate map of 1832 shows field boundaries little different from those drawn by Cogger in 1628. Many acres had been added in the meantime.

Under the settlement with the Ecclesiastical Commissioners, the Dean and Chapter made over to them not only the Court Lodge land, but also the Lordship of the Manor. The Commissioners became the third, and as it turned out, the last of the Lords of the Manor since the Saxon Kings gave the title to the Monks of Canterbury. The Lordship of the Manor for many years past had been of little profit to their predecessors, the Dean and Chapter. The rents collected from the principal tenants, holding their land for a fixed term, though ludicrously below the market value, had been worth collecting. The quit rents for the houses in the Street and on the Heath had not paid for the cost of collection. The collector's book for 1770 shows that after he had paid his expenses and the cost of a dinner to the tenants (essential if he was to collect their rents), there was no more than £1-9s.-6½d. to be paid into the coffers of the Chapter.

This was the heritage of the Ecclesiastical Commission. Oddly they still kept up the old practice of the Manor Court. A Court Baron was solemnly held every year at the Swan. A handful of trusties were induced by the hospitality offered to give attendance. As often as not their only business was to "amerce" all the tenants who had failed to attend to do their Homage. The fine of 1/- which they were amerced was, of course, never collected. Sometimes the Court did a little better. In law any sale of property in the Parish required the approval of the Manor. Nearly all such sales were in practice registered at the Court Baron, and a few pence came into the chest of the Commissioners.

After the Court Baron of 1927, the Clerk wrote into the book recording the transactions of the Court Baron, the heading for the next Court to be held in the following year. It was labour in vain. By then Lord Birkenhead's Act had been passed abolishing copyhold and all manorial rights and customs. The Manor of Appledore had come to an end. Few people in the village probably realised that an institution that had once been all powerful in the parish had silently come to its close.

12

NINETEENTH-CENTURY VILLAGE LIFE

The School, Tradesmen, Church and Chapel, Local Government.

The village community did not, of course, consist entirely of the farmers and their labourers, though they were far and away the largest section of the population. (This emerges very clearly in the 1841 census which is analysed in detail in Appendix V.) There were also the tradesmen and—the most permanent of all the dramatis personae—the Vicar.

The heyday of the tradesmen had been in medieval and Tudor times when Appledore was on the sea route and there was a weekly market in the village. As the sea link weakened and communications got worse, the trades preserved, at least, a monopoly of supply to all who lived in the parish. Not surprisingly *Bagshaw's Guide* of 1847 shows twenty tradesmen in Appledore. There was a butcher, two bakers, two grocers (both also drapers and one, Mr. Durrant, keeping the Post Office). There was a farrier, a saddler, two blacksmiths, three carpenters and three boot and shoemakers. Henry Crux, the miller, ran the two mills on the Heath, and there was a coal merchant. Elizabeth Packham kept a beerhouse, supplementing the Red Lion and the Swan. The railway came in 1851, and that was probably the cause of the two mills on the Heath falling into disuse. They were finally demolished in 1909. A sketch of the Union Mill is reproduced in Plate 8. The other trades however, continued to flourish, and—fifty years later—there are still 20 tradesmen in the list for 1897. There were now four grocers (two of them drapers as well), a butcher and a baker. The blacksmith was now supported by an ironmonger and a machinist. The carpenters had been taken over by two builders. There was only one boot store, but a saddler was still in business. In addition to Mrs. Green, listed as a higgler, there was a corn merchant, a carrier, a manure merchant and a man from the Pru. There were now four pubs, the Victoria and the Railway Inn competing with the Red Lion and the Swan. The former's days were numbered. The more attractive old building was demolished in the early 1930s and replaced by its modern successor. A photograph of the old inn is reproduced in Plate 10. Finally you could get board residence, if you wanted it, at Vine House.

It was not till the car and buses arrived that so many of the old village trades had to go out of business. The village is lucky still to have not only its four pubs but also its baker, two grocers and a champion blacksmith—and of course a large garage operated by the Bates family who once ran the barge service on the canal.

69

The Vicar of Appledore in the eighteenth century had been an absentee. The Pluralities Act of 1838 ensured that from then on the incumbent would live among his parishioners and play a full part in the community. After 1834 the seven vicars who spanned the rest of the century all lived in Appledore where a new vicarage (now the old vicarage!) replaced the picturesque but tumbledown old building of the fifteenth century. In its latter days this house had turned into a series of squalid tenements. In 1815 the Churchwardens were instructed by the Vestry to make regular applications to the Archbishop "On account of the numerous families residing in the Vicarage House, which is considered an injustice to the Parish".

The last of the vicars appointed under the old system chose voluntarily to live in his parish. The Rev. William Dixon wore the traditional shovel hat, black round coat, knee breeches and stockings—the last to do so in Appledore. His second wife was a Munk and both of them took to the bottle. His ever shakier signature in the vestry book bears witness to the hold it had on him. He had finally to be moved from the Parish. From then on the Archbishop appointed men who not only served the parish well but in a number of cases were of high calibre and went on to promotion in other church appointments.

Not surprisingly, it was during Mr. Dixon's time that the Wesleyan Chapel was built in Appledore in 1836. It filled a need and revived the old tradition of non-conformity. Not only did the Vicars provide full and conscientious pastoral service. They carried out with energy, sometimes with more energy than taste, a thorough restoration of the fabric of the church. Appendix VII describes what they did in this field. Appendix VIII deals with the restoration of the bells by their successors.

Another by-product of Mr. Dixon's unfortunate condition was his employment of a curate. One of them, the Rev. F. Goold, should always be remembered in Appledore with the greatest gratitude. On November 21st, 1840, he founded the present village school. It was not the first time there had been a school in the village. The grammar school for which William Brokhill made provision in his will of 1519 may not have been set up. There is, however, a certificate signed in 1662 by the Vicar of Appledore, Francis Drayton, testifying that "Mr. William Graves is of a good conversation and of good ability to teach a school" This was endorsed "I give my consent that Mr. William Graves teach school at Appledore". At that time, at any rate, there was schooling to be had. Indeed schooling in the church may have been provided from then on because, when the north chapel was repaired in 1700, it was shut off from the rest of the church by a partition of lathe and plaster mounted on studding. (The mortices for this can be seen in the top of the screen.) Certainly by the start of the nineteenth century this was where the school was, and in all probability this was where Mary Harman taught. It is rare to find any note in the Registers about those whose births, deaths and marriages are recorded. When, however, in

1787, Mrs. Harman was buried, the curate wrote a tribute to her in Latin. Translated it reads: "Alas what a loss to the village. For twenty years and more she fulfilled her duty as a teacher with the utmost devotion. How well, all those living in the parish testify, she knew how to instil literacy in the young."

This school in the church was evidently subsidised by the Vestry from the Poor Rate, but the first time this is mentioned in the surviving records was when in 1820 the annual grant of £5 for educating poor children was discontinued. Notice was then also given of a resolution "to shut up the school in the church". That was not its end. It is known that for some years at least it was continued in the long room of the house that is now the bakery.

There was, then, some sort of education in the village in the seventeenth, eighteenth and early nineteenth centuries, but, in 1840, Mr. Goold, the curate, introduced a new era in the village by setting up the school which still provides Primary education for Appledore. He must have been a man of great drive and energy for he had to secure not only a building and a schoolmaster but the funds to keep it in being. This he did by getting subscriptions and by preaching fund-raising sermons in the church.

A feature of the school which lasted right through the nineteenth century was that the parents had to pay a 1d. a week for each child attending. This payment was required even after attendance was made compulsory. The "pence" formed an important part of the school-master's salary. They were an incentive for him to secure the attendance of his pupils, but the charge must have meant a sacrifice for many parents. The schoolmaster had, moreover, to work against the counter-attraction of work for children in the hop gardens and potato fields, and the attendance figures were often low.

The school was opened in the building (now enlarged) where it still is. In the early years this was rented for £5 a year from Mr. Zion Adams. After 1851 there are no further entries for rent, and the building must have been acquired by gift or purchase.

The schoolmaster's salary of £10 was not princely. Still less was that of the sempstress at £5. The schoolmaster, however, got his house and garden and the "pence". These were no more than 5/- a week in 1851, but that doubled his salary. From this payment it can be deduced that some 60 children were then going to school. The accounts were kept a little eccentrically, but in 1851 they totalled £37 13s. 0d., including 5/- for the use of towels and £1 for stationery. In the year before 6½d. had been spent on slate pencils, so that the stationery was not used extravagantly.

The early years were dogged by difficulty in raising funds, particularly for repairing and extending the building. Far harder was how to retain a schoolmaster for more than a year on end. One at least left because he got too friendly with the sempstress. Some may have resigned because Appledore was still not a very healthy place. As late as 1860, when advertising the post, the Governors thought it wise to mention that ague was prevalent in the parish. By that year the salary had been raised to £20, plus the pence, which in the previous year had brought in a further £35. This compared very well with the emoluments of many curates with higher qualifications. Eventually Mr. John Jarvis, appointed in 1869, settled in the post and was still serving in 1904—a long and faithful period of service. His appointment came at the right time. H.M. Inspector of Schools had just reported that the school was "thoroughly inefficient". No further complaints about the standards were made in Mr. Jarvis's time, and in 1887 the report was "very satisfactory". It is said that in the year before "owing to the continued depression in trade and agriculture" Mr. Jarvis had his salary reduced. It still came to £100, inclusive of pence, but it was a reduction from £109 the year before. This blow, moreover, followed a reduction of £8 in 1882.

There were 150 children on the books in 1860. The main need was then and in later years to get more regular attendance. The other trouble was still money. By 1881 annual expenditure was running at £155 and in the agricultural depression it became harder to raise voluntary subscriptions and quite impossible to finance any improvements. These were urgently needed. The inspector's reports year after year mention bad ventilation and a need for "new class room and proper offices". Poor Mr. Jarvis was instructed to supervise the management of the earth closets, but the extensions could not be put off any longer.

The school got two windfalls. In 1859 the Dean and Chapter decided to enclose the remaining open area of the Heath. This by rights was for the benefit of the parishioners. In a fit of generosity the Dean and Chapter allocated 9 acres to the school for a quit rent of 1/- a year. This was let for £22 a year to Jacob Kingsnorth. His rent was a very useful addition to the school revenues. In 1886 he asked for and got a reduction of 15% "owing to the depression in the trade and agriculture". This was a turn of the wheel for the overseer of the poor who not so long before had handed out the dole to the labourers. At least he didn't have to submit to a means test!

The other windfall came from the decision of the Vestry to apply £243 of the proceeds of the sale of Poor Row for the benefit of the school. This was opposed by the serried ranks of Bumbledom in Tenterden and Whitehall, but the Vestry persisted and won. Nearly £300 had to be spent on extensions and improvements in 1874. The Diocese gave £60, the National Society £12 and a 9d. rate was raised in the parish. The Poor Row money found £134. The balance of £109 was used in 1893 for repairs and alterations. The interest meanwhile under a decision of the Bumbles had been used in a reduction of the Union poor rate.

One dashing innovation in management was made in 1874. Ladies were put on the Visiting Committee. Mrs. Poile, the wife of a member of a long established Ebony family, was the pioneer of Women's Lib in this field.

By current standards the school was gravely overcrowded and grossly understaffed, but Appledore had every reason to be grateful for its foundation and continued existence. Mr. Jarvis's schooling opened the way for new employments and a wider life for many of the children who came under his care.

Local government in and by the parish was meanwhile in decay. The Parish Vestry had for two centuries, with the local J.P.s, exercised most of the activities of government in the parish. Interventions by central government had been rare. In the Napoleonic war they had sent the army into the parish and lodged them in barracks at Redhill. They had also used compulsory powers (for which they had doubtful statutory authority) to take the land required to build the canal. The Excise men waged ceaseless war on the smugglers, but in general it was the Vestry which governed the parish. They appointed and paid the Parish Constable his salary of £2. They raised a gaol rent to pay for the prison at Dymchurch. In so far as anyone did, they maintained the roads with local labour, levying a highway rate to pay the cost. The parish overseers, at first unpaid and only towards the end receiving a pittance, had to dispense the poor relief, enforce the law of settlement and go with the constable to the magistrate to deal with malefactors. They were also the government's agents for assessing and collecting the property tax. All this came to an end with the Act of 1834 and the Vestry proceedings from then on became largely formal. More and more, apart from raising the poor rate, they tended to confine their work to what was purely church business. In 1868 they were given powers by statute to dispense with one more of their customary functions—the raising of the church rate to pay for the upkeep of the church and churchyard. The practice, however, died hard in Appledore. As late as 1889 a church rate of 1d. in the £ was levied, but a number of parishioners showed their disapproval by noting their payments as "donations". No further church rate was raised. The appointment of the Rev. E. B. Russell in that year may have had something to do with the decision.

The Vestry continued to appoint the constable and to pay him his salary of £2. His powers and authority are not apparent, but as late as 1822 the Parish Stocks were still in use. In that year the Vestry had ordered them to be set up "next to Mr. Benjamin Blinks open shamels shop". Sometime later they were moved outside Court Lodge, where they crumbled into decay in the eighties.

So did the Vestry. The President of the Local Government Board, introducing the Local Government Bill, described the vestries as "decrepit survivals of former days with the form but not the powers of local government". When the bill became law in 1894 the Vestry ceased to exist except as a church organisation and in that year, the Parish Council, which took its place, held its first meeting.

One of the first problems of the new council was that of the annual fair. This had taken place every year since the right to hold it had been granted by Edward III. The Dean and Chapter, as Lords of the Manor who had received the grant, had had no difficulty in getting a tenant of the fair. He paid a nominal sum, and after meeting the salary of the Bailiff, may have made a small profit out of the dues paid by the stall holders. As early as 1834 the Vestry were getting worried by the Fair. Four special constables were appointed for a sum of 10d. apiece to reinforce the constable and the bailiff "in consequences of disturbances by idle and disorderly persons at the Fair". By the end of the century it seems that the vagabonds and gypsies who came in were getting out of hand and in 1898 they decided to "take decisive steps for the abolition of the Annual Fair as now held in Appledore Street". Next year an Order in Council was made to abolish the fair and a 600-year-old institution came to an end. Mr. Venis, who built the houses next to the Post Office, had the melancholy satisfaction of being the last of the bailiffs, the last successor of the first bailiff of the Manor. He had worn a blue uniform with brass buttons, rather like that still worn by the Sergeant to the Lords of the Level of Romney Marsh, and he carried a staff of office. The staff is still preserved.

Another, but easier task for the Council was to take over the management of the allotments which had been a great institution in the village since 1837. The idea of allotments as a means of reducing the misery of unemployed or underpaid labourers had been put forward in the early eighteenth century by many reformers up and down the country. They had met with opposition from the Government, and in many villages from the farmers. Appledore was more enlightened. In 1835 a letter was sent to the Dean and Chapter urging an "allotment system". The letter was signed by sixteen members of the Vestry headed by the Vicar, the Rev. William Dixon. The system, they suggested, had been shown to have had "beneficial effects for the Labouring Poor. It not only produces the necessaries of life but enables them to bring children up with industrious habits and will eventually restore that feeling of Independence and good Morals which formerly characterised the English Peasantry". A scheme, if introduced, "would add to the comforts of the Industrious Poor".

The Dean and Chapter were involved as Lords of the Manor. They owned the Heath, which was manorial waste and under manorial custom common land which all parishioners could graze and from which they could gather firing. Encroachments had occurred from time to time. These took the form of enclosing land with hedges or even building houses on the enclosures. Some had been recognised by the Manor. Others had just happened and the Manor had no means or real incentive to dispossess the squatters. One enclosure of fifteen acres had indeed been made by the Overseers to provide a Parish

Farm on which the Paupers could be set to work. This was on the "Lower Heath" fronting on Moor Lane where the land falls away to the level of Shirley Moor. The promoters suggested this as the site of the allotments.

The Dean and Chapter, or their advisers, saw the chance of a bargain. They would graciously agree to the 15 acres, which were in fact, under the custom of the Manor, for the use of the parishioners, being enclosed and turned into allotments, but they made it a condition that the Management Committee should secure the removal of thirteen encroachments which they listed. The Committee carried out the bargain—or at any rate part of it. The pitiful shacks which some of the squatters had put up were pulled down. Compensation was paid in some, but not all, cases. The unfortunate Solomon Giles was one of those evicted. 14/7d. was paid for the small beer drunk by the labourers who pulled down his shack. In other cases the squatter got away with it. James Macket Paine had built a house. This was not pulled down. The Committee did no more than deprive him of his allotment and even this penalty was revoked after some years. His house remains today—the attractive house, known as Heath Cottage, next to the school playing field.

Meanwhile 37 out of the 58 applicants had been granted an allotment of a rood (a quarter of an acre) apiece. Twenty-seven of them could not sign their names and had to make their mark. The signatures of the remaining 31 are a tribute to the schooling given in the school in the church. They paid 2/- a year rent. One shilling had been suggested by the promoters. The Dean and Chapter had doubled this. Occupiers had also, reasonably enough, to keep the rules which were printed and given to all those who had secured an allotment.

One, at any rate, of the rules was far from reasonable. "All occupiers will be expected to attend regularly at some place of worship on the Sabbath day together with their family." Four men, in the early days of the system, were actually given notice to quit for breaking this rule. Later they were allowed back on undertaking to do better in future. Another condition was that only the spade was to be used for turning the soil. The use of the plough or any other machinery was forbidden. A number of occupants who were idle enough to borrow horses and tackle to ease their own backs lost their allotment. The provision was symptomatic of the attitude of the farmers to the labouring poor. At all costs they must be kept in the ranks of the "Industrious Poor". Give them a chance and they might lapse into idle "Rogues and Vagabonds".

For some reason not explained there were never more than 10 acres laid out in allotments for 44 occupiers. Four acres of land were at first cropped by the Committee and the standing crop sold by auction. This may have been done to provide work and get some extra revenue for the "system". Later the 4 acre field and the green lanes leading to the allotments were let for grazing.

By 1837 the "Allotment System" had been restyled the Appledore Labourers Friendly Society. Their annual accounts show that they were able to balance their books and each year provide an annual dinner at 1/6d. a head and a cash bonus of 6d. or 1/-.

The original Committee of Management was formed by farmers holding Manor land. They filled their vacancies by cooption. There was no question of democratic elections or representation of allotment holders on the Committee. Nor was there any suggestion that this self perpetuating oligarchy abused its position. At one point indeed in 1838 they suggested to the Dean and Chapter that the rest of the Heath might be enclosed. They had had trouble enough in ejecting squatters and unless the rest of the land was enclosed "there will be continual trouble to prevent encroachments and attempts to do this create unpleasant feeling in the parish". The Dean and Chapter's advisers knew how to deal with this suggestion. They asked how the legal problem was to be tackled and the suggestion was dropped. It was not till 1859 that the rest of the Heath was enclosed. The suggestion of the Committee was not entirely altruistic. As existing tenants they were likely to be allotted any further land enclosed.

The allotments continued to be an undoubted boon to the 42 allotment holders. The rules were observed. Holders were ejected for bad husbandry or when they became tradesmen or property owners. By the late 60s the "non-natives" who had lived for up to five years in the parish were admitted but there was no suggestion of any lack of applicants.

In 1894 the Parish Council was set up. The Committee, advised that there was no legal compulsion for them to give up office, at first carried on. Three years later they decided to transfer the allotments and their management to the Council. Under the new management two more generations were to enjoy these smallholdings. Then the demand fell away—a welcome indication of greater prosperity.

It is hard to form a general picture of conditions in the parish in this century. At its start they could hardly have been worse for the great majority. The population, despite emigration, was increasing. Numbers rose from 384 in 1801 to 568 in 1831. By 1851 it was 621 and a peak of 671 was reached in 1871. From then to the turn of the century, it started to fall away again. The agricultural depression, disastrous to many farmers, brought a reduction in employment and wages, but at least food was far cheaper, and the railway, available since 1851, gave scope for work in Ashford. Education, firmly established at the school, was reducing illiteracy. Working on the land was no longer the only job for which the new generation were qualified.

Health was undoubtedly better. The increase in the population is the best evidence. Already by the end of the century the village was to see the arrival in the Street of a new category of resident—people coming to live in Appledore in their retirement—a clear proof that the ague was no longer frightening people away.

Appledore like all other villages had to go through the 1914 and 1939 wars and, especially in the first war, to see some of the best of her young men sacrificed. The two wars can never be remembered except as calamities, but improvements followed them. Local government was able to build the houses that had been so badly lacking in the nineteenth century. The new social services provided for unemployment, sickness and old age. There are no longer the Two Nations in Appledore that had been so tragically separated in the years of poverty. A new and better balanced community has taken its place. You can still enjoy the charm of the Street which has changed so little over the centuries. You can look out almost anywhere from a house in the Street or on the Heath to the lovely landscape of the Marsh, or to the view of Ebony or Oxney. You can do this no longer troubled by the thought that in most of these houses the thought once always uppermost was whether there would be enough food for the next day. Some things have changed for the better.

EPILOGUE

The topographers who have mentioned Appledore in their works, from Philipot down to Hasted, have filled their pages with accounts of the noble families connected with the parish. Very few of them lived in it. For most of them Appledore was a place where they held an investment of land which provided part of their fortune. This concentration by authors on the notables is understandable since they were then the only people likely to buy the books. Few of their readers would be interested to read about the men and women of the village who lived the whole of their lives there. Even the monk who wrote the Anglo Saxon Chronicle, refers to the brave men who manned their half-built earthwork against the Danish invaders as a few churls, and no one knows their names. Only two of those who fought against tyranny in the great risings of 1381 and 1450 have left their names on record. Of all the ten thousand who have been buried in the churchyard a large part lie unnamed. Those who are recorded in the Registers are nearly all just names. Nothing more is known about them. But they were the people of Appledore. Without them there would be no village. Perhaps those who now plough the same fields, live where they lived and even bear their names, as they read this account may recall the words written of another churchyard:

"Let not ambition mock their useful toil,
Their homely joys, and destiny obscure;
Nor Grandeur hear with a disdainful smile
The short and simple annals of the poor."

NOTES ON SOURCES

(Abbreviations on page iv)

Chapter 1

For theories about the original course of the Rother delta see
A.C.13 particularly Robert Furley's article on page 178. The outlet
from Appledore to Romney and Greatstone is abundantly proven, as
is the outlet from Appledore to Rye. The third outlet from Appledore
to Lympne is more conjectural. It is clear that at Appledore at least
two and possibly three outlets branched out from the main Rother
channel from Bodiam and Smallhythe.

The Mithraic altar at Stone in Oxney is described in the note on
the church there by W. H. Yeandle (Church Army Press, 1935). See
also Dr. Cock's article in A.C.47. For Roman pottery at Dymchurch
see Furley, op. cit.

The origin of diggings on the hill behind Court Lodge is given in a
note by Dr. Cock. His family were tenants of the farm at the time
(1840).

Chapter 2

The only reliable source for Haesten's raid is the A.S. Chronicle.
A discussion of the "myth" of the stone castle at Appledore is given
in Appendix II. The charters quoted are all in the Library of
Canterbury Cathedral.

Chapter 3

The list of the Archbishop's tenants by knight service in about
1170 is quoted on page 15 of vol. XVIII of *Kent Records of Mediaeval
Kentish Society* published by the Kentish Archaeological Society in 1964

All the manor records referred to are in the Library of Canterbury
Cathedral.

The main protagonist of an earlier date for the north chapel is Dr.
Cock (see earlier editions of the church guide). Compare however the
note by Mr. F. C. Elliston—Erwood F.S.A. on pp. 103-5 of Archaeologia
Cantiana vol. 64 *Kilburn's Topography*, 1659, gives the date of the Frenc
raid as 10 August, 1380.

For the survival of serfdom in Kent see A.C. Vol. 12, p. 283 et seq.
The documents dealing with the blocking of the Rhee Channel and
the efforts to keep it open are quoted in A.C. Vol. 13, p. 261 et seq.
The events of 1377-1380 are described in Thomas of Walsingham's
History in the Rolls Series. The discovery of the embers in the N.W.
corner of the nave was recorded by Dr. Cock in 1925. (See Appendix
VII.)

The causes of the 1381 risings and the summary of its development
are given in G. M. Trevelyan's *England in the age of Wycliff*— 1899

The appointment of William Horne on July 20th, 1381, is referred
to in A.C. Vol. 3, p. 69. On page 78 op. cit. is a translation of the

indictment of William of Apuldre, and an account of the raid on Hornes Place. For John Onewynes' attack on Hornes Place on June 17th see the Ancient Indictment quoted in the Appendix to G. M. Trevelyan op. cit. published by Trevelyan and Powell. Dalyngrigge's reconstitution of the manorial records is referred to in Réville's *Soulevement des Travailleurs anglais en 1381*. The beheading of William Apuldre de Malling comes in the escheator's accounts quoted by Réville. A translation of the curious affair of September 30th, 1381, in which Philip of Apuldre was involved is given in A.C. Vol. 4 on p. 75 et. seq.

Chapter 4

The account of Wycliff's activities is founded on G. M. Trevelyan, op. cit. The incidents recorded in Appledore from 1428 to 1450 are from documents quoted in *The later Lollards* by John Thomson, OUP, 1965. The pardons for all the contingents from Kent taking part in Jack Cade's rising—for acts committed up to July 7th, 1450— are reproduced in A.C. Vol. 7, pp. 233 et. seq. John Claydych's pardon is in Cal. Patent Rolls 30 Henry VI, p. 497.

For another of William Parmenter's reconnaissances in force see *Kent Records* (Vol. 18) published by the K.A.S. on page 253.

All the wills are in the P.C.C. William Marshall's highly interesting will of 1523 is reproduced in full in A.C. Vol. 43.

Hasted (1798 edition) Vol. VII on page 246 says that Roger Horne acquired Kenardington Manor 24 Henry VIII. On page 256 he says that they removed to Kenardington in the reign of Henry VII on purchasing the manor there.

The catalogue of the lights in the church is compiled from entries in contemporary wills. The description of the stained glass windows is from an entry in the old Register (lost since the eighteenth century) copied into the oldest surviving register dating from 1700. This entry is reproduced in A.C. Vol. 14. The 1700 entry records that the east window was then still surviving.

Chapter 5

Roger and Henry Horne's deaths and testamentary provisions are recorded in inquests dated October 24th, 1544, and June 26th, 1566.

The information about Philip Chute is drawn from Dr. Cock's article in A.C. Vol. 49 and from Philip Chute's will in the P.C.C. An inquest of 1590 which may refer to Horne's Place is also referred to in this article. Philip Chute died on 5th April, 1567. See my note in A.C. Vol. XCV, page 290.

The information about the leases of the Court Lodge and its land comes from the manorial records at Canterbury. The rebuilding of Court Lodge by Prior Goldstone is given in a note to Willis's *Mitred Abbeys* quoted by Hasted Vol. VII, page 255.

For the carriage of timber to Dover see Additional MSS, 34147, page 109. For land management in Appledore see my article in A. C. Vol. XCVII, page 1.

Chapter 6

Cranmer's wife and her travelling box are mentioned in the article on Thomas Cranmer in D.N.B. The destruction of the mass books, etc., at Appledore in 1550 is mentioned in A.C. Vol. 31, pages 104-5 (aboliti fuerunt).

The sale of the church silver for 19/4d. is recorded in Sir John Guldeforde's certificate P.R.O. E117/11/39. Thomas de Marynes penance (or rather the fine he paid in lieu)is recorded in A.C. Vol. 32, pp. 144 and 164.

Chapter 7

The statement that the Red Lion was originally on the west side of the Street rests on a statement of Edward Avery recorded by Dr. Cock.

Chapter 8

The 1827 figures of absentee clergy are given in *The Victorian Church* (A. & C. Black, 1966) Part I, p. 34. The 1769 Map is reproduced by H. Margary, Lympne Castle, Kent, in 1968. Penance in Cambridgeshire in 1849 is recorded in *The Victorian Church* (op. cit.) p. 489.

Chapter 9

Most of the information given in this chapter is taken from the article in the *Army Quarterly* of October 1953 by Professor Richard Glover and in the lecture by Lt.-Col. C. H. Lemmon, D.S.O., published by the Rye Art Association in 1963.

The 1794 invasion plan is described in papers given to Dr. Cock by Col. Curteis of Tenterden.

Chapter 10

The facts come almost entirely from the surviving Overseers' accounts 1792 to 1801 and 1812 to 1819 and the Vestry Book 1815-1823 and 1830 to 1908 now in the County Archives Office at Maidstone. On the Speenhamland System see *The Village Labourer* by J. L. and B. Hammond, Longmans, 1927. For the price of wheat see *A Century of Agricultural Statistics,* H.M.S.O., 1968.

Chapter 11

The facts about the Munks are from a MS history of the family. The tithe assessments are from the awards in the County Archive Office. The later Manor records are in the Cathedral Library. The 1832 Map of the Chute estate is in the County Archives Office.

Appendix I

THE DERIVATION OF THE
PLACE NAME OF APPLEDORE

Apuldre is the name written in all the early Saxon charters and in the Anglo-Saxon chronicle itself. This spelling continued right into the fourteenth and fifteenth centuries, when the present "dore" began to be adopted. There are three main theories about the derivation of the name.

The first and simplest is that it is just the Saxon word for appletree, which it is. For example, in the A.S.C. description of the battle of Hastings, it is the har apuldre—the hoary appletree—which Harold chooses as his muster point. William Somner—a great authority on the Anglo-Saxon language—in his *Roman Ports and Forts,* is against this derivation, but partly, at any rate, for horticultural reasons, on the ground that the appletree is a "plant for which the soil is nothing proper nor scarce for any other". He is scarcely fair to Appledore. Even if the undrained marshes in Saxon times were totally unsuitable for fruit trees, an appletree could have grown on the upland as well then as now and could have become a landmark. The simple "appletree" derivation is not to be rejected. Any Saxon hearing the word would at once have thought of the fruit tree.

A second theory is that preferred by Somner. He thinks it was originally spelt Aet puldre—the place of the polder. He argues that from early times land was reclaimed from the sea by inning, i.e. by throwing up banks to keep out the sea, and that the reclaimed land was known as a "polder", as indeed it still is in Holland. He cites a place near Canterbury called a polder. He might indeed have found in an early mediaeval charter a field name in Appledore, itself called Twypolder. The prefix "aet", as he points out, is common in Saxon place names and in time equally commonly the prefix was absorbed into the main word.

The third theory assumes that the place already had a Celtic name before the Jutish invasion and that the Jutes took it over and Saxonised the word. The key syllable under this theory is the final "re" which, it is claimed, is the same as "Rhee" in the Rhee Wall. The letter "d" may have come in by mistaken Saxon theories that the word meant appletree. The "pul" would represent the Celtic pol = head; and the "A" would be the Saxon aet. The complete word would therefore indicate "the place at the head of the "Rhee Wall" (or the Rhee channel).

A variant of the Celtic place name theory is "apul dwyr" = the confluence of the streams.

81

Appendix II

THE MYTH OF APPLEDORE CASTLE

Two myths repeated by successive topographers whose works have touched on Appledore are, I believe, without foundation.

The first is that a castle (built of stone) was built at Appledore by Haesten as a base for his campaign in 892.

The second is that this castle survived till it was demolished by the French in the course of their raid on Appledore in 1380 and that Appledore Church was built out of the stonework left on the site.

Haesten almost certainly built a strong point at Appledore as a base for the main part of the fleet which he left there in 892 and in the language spoken after 1066 this was called a "castle". In Saxon times it would have been referred to as a "geweorc", which more adequately describes the earthworks which both Saxons and Danes threw up in the time of King Alfred. Such "castles" are still known as such in other places in Kent, for example, Castle Rough at Milton-on-Swale which was also built by Haesten to protect the detachment of 80 ships which he sent there from Appledore. The surviving texts of the Anglo-Saxon Chronicle do not in so many words say that Haesten built an earthwork at Appledore but there is a strong implication in the narrative that he did. Florence of Worcester (who died in 1118) may have had another text of the Chronicle which has since been lost. After referring to the destruction by the Danes of the half-built fort held by local peasants, he says that the Danes threw up for themselves a stronger one at a place called Appledore. Henry of Huntington also is definite about a Danish strongpoint at Appledore "construxerunt castrum apud Awldre".

There is absolutely no reason to doubt that Haesten built an earthwork, revetted with turf and fenced by a palisade of stakes, to protect his longships and the "island" of Appledore is as likely a site as any since there was the meeting place of the two channels—to Romney and Rye—both of which had to be watched.

The myth of the stonebuilt Danish castle, surviving for five hundred years only to be destroyed by the French in 1380, does not appear in Stow, Holinshed or Camden. In 1659 two topographers mention the legend. Thomas Philipott's *Kent Surveyed* starts by introducing a second Danish invasion in the reign of King Ethelred (not mentioned in the A.S.C.) which led to the destruction of Haesten's castle and its replacement by a second Danish castle. This he says survived and was included in the "castles and fortresses of this country until 1380 when the French raid reduced it to a heap of flame and ruin out of whose dismantled reliques the church now visible was not only repaired, but, as some from ancient tradition affirm, wholly re-edified, a probable argument of the ancient grandeur, magnificence and strength of this totally demolished fortress." *Kilburn's Topography* published in the same year, omits the second Danish raid but says of Haesten's castle "what became of it afterwards I find not only is it probable that it was ruined by the French who on 10th August 1380 burned the town, and by tradition, upon the ruins of that castle the present church was builded".

Two later topographers repeat the same story. Charles Seymour's *Survey of Kent*, 1776, repeats the story of the raid in King Ethelred's time and goes on to say that the second Danish castle was deemed one of the strongest castles and fortresses in this country, "as appears by the Register, till the French demolished it, and on its site the present church was built". Hasted in 1798 after saying that the church before 1380 stood in a field adjoining Redhill Bridge, takes up the tale that the present church was built on the site of the ancient castle demolished by the French in 1380, "the ruins furnishing many materials for the building of it".

Later writers copy their predecessors including Holloway in 1859 in his *history of Romney Marsh*.

Whoever it was who started the legend of the church built from the remains of the ancient Danish castle, he cannot have studied the architecture of Appledore church. The north chapel, the chancel, the arches of the nave and tower were built well over a century before 1380. Moreover, when the floor of the nave was relaid in 1925, masses of embers were found to confirm the evidence of the fire reddened arches of the north door and west arch and prove that the Early English Church was severely damaged by fire. It is totally impossible that the church was first built in 1380. It is fully proven that the earlier church was damaged by fire and it is highly probable that this fire occurred as a result of the French raid in 1380.

It is, of course, possible that in Appledore some kind of stone fortification had been built before 1380, that this was destroyed by the French and its materials used in the repair or enlargement of the church after 1380. If so it was certainly not built by Danish raiders, who had neither the time nor the skill to make such fortifications.

Appendix III

APPLEDORE AND THE BATTLE OF HASTINGS

Both Furley and Sandys state that Harold mustered his forces to meet William at the estuary of Appledore. I have not followed them and draw attention to their statements only, as I hope, to refute them.

Furley (*History of the Weald of Kent*, 1871, Vol. 1, page 210) relies on what he says is Gale's edition of the A.S.C. which, he claims, says that "Harold met his army at the estuary of Appledore". Furley adds his own gloss on this by suggesting that he more probably "assembled his army at the estuary of Appledore". Sandys' *Gavelkind* (1851) quotes an alleged extract from the A.S.C. "Harold came to meet him (William) at the estuary of Appledore."

Neither Furley nor Sandys give the A.S. text and Sandys does not give the author of the English version on which he relies. The well known edition of the A.S.C. by the Rev. J. Ingram (London, 1823), a copy of which is in the Library of Canterbury Cathedral, may be the source of their story. The relevant passage of the text and its parallel translation is "He gaderade tha mycelne here. Com him togener aet thaera haran Apuldran. He (Harold) gathered a large force and came to meet him (William) at the estuary of Appledore". It seems possible that both Furley and Sandys relied on Ingram's version. This is clearly a mistranslation of the Saxon text. "Har apuldre" means the hoary appletree—perhaps a tree covered with lichen. Aet takes the dative case in both the adjective and noun. The phrase cannot be translated "at the estuary of Appledore". There is not even the possibility that Ingram had access to a text which is now lost. The only surviving text of the A.S.C. which has any account of the Battle of Hastings is MS "D" which is virtually identical with Ingram's "Harold cyng . . . gaderade tha mycelne here, com him to genes aet thaera haran apuldran. Wyllem him com ongean on unwaer aer his folc gefylced waere". King Harold gathered a numerous army and came to oppose him at the hoary appletree. William came upon him unawares before his people were set in order. The chronicle goes on "and the king fought against him most heartily with those of his men who were willing to stand by him. There was great slaughter. King Harold, Earl Leofwine his brother, Earl Gurth his brother and many good men were slain. The French had possession of the place of slaughter, as God granted because of the nations sins".

The suggestion that the Appledore estuary was Harold's muster ground has, therefore, no foundation. It would indeed have been a most misguided choice except for any of the Fyrd who may have come by sea. The "hoary" appletree seems, admittedly, a vague enough direction to the muster ground. Col. Lemmon, however, in his article on the battle in *The Norman Conquest* (Eyre & Spottiswood, 1966) sees no difficulty in identifying the spot as Caldbec Hill to the north of the battlefield or to there having been an appletree on its top which would have been a local landmark.

Furley (op. cit.) also refers to an incident near Appledore after the battle. He quotes Lingard (Vol. 1, page 218) as saying that William's first move after the battle was to Romney where he severely chastised the inhabitants for their valour in repelling his invading army. Hasted gives a rather more accurate version, quoting William of Poitiers, William's chaplain, as his source. The raid he explains was to revenge the death at the hands of the men of Romney of some of his men, who had landed there in the invasion.

William's punitive force, if it went to Romney on foot, could have passed through Appledore. Col. Lemmon (op. cit.) has ingeniously identified those places in Kent on the route of William's march from Battle to Dover which suffered from pillage, by comparing the values shown in Domesday at the time of the survey and in the reign of Edward the Confessor. His theory is that a marked fall in value points to pillage in 1066. This test is inconclusive for Appledore. "In the time of King Edward it was taxed at two sulings and now for one." On the other hand "the church, the fishery, two acres of meadow and wood pannage for six hogs was worth £6 in the time of King Edward, now £16 17 6."

Appendix IV

STATISTICS OF CHRISTENINGS,
MARRIAGES AND BURIALS
AT APPLEDORE, 1563 - 1812

Year	C	M	B	Year	C	M	B
1563	9	7	37	1601	14	5	16
1566	10	2	11	1602	10	6	7
1567	6	4	6	1603	16	5	14
1568	11	4	33	1604	def	5	6
1569	12	5	23	1605	def	def	def
1570	12	12	25	1606	3	5	def
1571	15	5	29	1607	19	3	21
1572	17	1	19	1608	def	4	def
1573	13	7	12	1609	9	5	24
1574	10	5	12	1610	7	nil	18
1575	13	4	10	1611	5	2	21
1576	17	3	9	1612	4	7	8
1577	9	4	4	1613	4	5	22
1578	10	3	13	1614	5	2	13
1579	11	5	9	1615	6	3	15
1580	13	3	26	1616	7	2	10
1581	12	4	22	1617	7	3	16
1582	7	3	21	1618	12	2	14
1583	11	10	24	1619	7	4	12
1584	def	def	def	1620	17	2	18
1585	def	def	def	1621	4	3	4
1586	8	1	16	1622	13	3	19
1587	7	3	3	1623	8	3	12
1588	8	2	11	1624	14	1	24
1589	13	2	10	1625	5	6	17
1590	5	8	21	1626	8	1	10
1591	11	4	23	1627	9	7	16
1592	10	9	22	1628	15	10	17
1593	8	3	22	1629	14	9	15
1594	def	def	def	1630	3	nil	16
1595	def	def	def	1631	5	2	18
1596	def	def	10	1632	14	5	13
1597	6	3	14	1633	8	2	6
1598	13	6	14	1634	19	8	11
1599	8	10	12	1635	12	6	15
1600	16	8	20	1636	17	4	25

Year	C	M	B	Year	C	M	B
1637	15	5	29	1701	3	1	22
1638	16	7	36	1702	6	1	14
1639	13	7	22	1703	10	nil	13
1640	17	8	33	1704	5	2	11
1641	7	2	23	1704	4	1	15
1642-				1706	9	4	16
1661		No records		1707	8	2	11
1662	9	3	16	1708	7	3	12
1663	15	1	10	1709	4	2	11
1664	10	1	15	1710	10	2	9
1665	14	nil	37	1711	14	2	5
1666	8	nil	19	1712	11	1	15
1667	10	1	39	1713	10	4	8
1668	8	2	15	1714	9	5	7
1669	6	6	23	1715	17	nil	8
1670	9	3	15	1716	14	3	9
1671	7	3	19	1717	8	2	10
1672	7	2	12	1718	8	1	7
1673	7	3	3	1719	10	2	23
1674	10	4	8	1720	9	3	22
1675	8	4	7	1721	13	1	16
1676	12	2	18	1722	10	3	12
1677	8	4	14	1723	15	1	5
1678	7	2	21	1724	9	3	10
1679	4	2	19	1725	10	1	7
1680	9	1	10	1726	7	3	5
1681	4	2	23	1727	11	1	17
1682	9	7	11	1728	4	1	7
1683	11	2	9	1729	8	1	9
1684	7	3	8	1730	4	1	8
1685	3	2	8	1731	10	2	6
1686	13	1	13	1732	10	3	12
1687	9	2	13	1733	10	2	11
1688	14	3	12	1734	7	2	7
1689	5	5	7	1735	9	3	11
1690	4	1	9	1736	6	1	8
1691	10	nil	13	1737	10	1	15
1692	4	nil	11	1738	6	2	8
1693	8	3	13	1739	11	1	6
1694	11	4	7	1740	9	3	2
1695	4	1	nil	1741	8	1	16
1696	11	nil	6	1742	11	2	8
1697	6	1	1	1743	7	nil	12
1698	8	2	nil	1744	12	nil	7
1699	9	nil	5	1745	4	2	7
1700	9	4	5	1746	10	3	6

Year	C	M	B	Year	C	M	B
1747	5	2	6	1780	8	2	13
1748	4	1	3	1781	11	5	11
1749	4	1	3	1782	13	2	9
1749	7	1	10	1783	10	2	2
1750	8	nil	8	1784	13	nil	7
1751*	6	1	7	1785	13	4	4
1752	8	2	8	1786	12	2	4
1753	7	2	2	1787	16	3	10
1754	10	1	8	1788	9	6	9
1755	7	1	4	1789	17	6	2
1756	9	1	5	1790	15	2	10
1757	8	3	7	1791	12	3	6
1758	10	3	5	1792	16	1	5
1759	3	2	5	1793	14	3	5
1760	9	2	5	1794	8	3	3
1761	7	6	7	1795	18	1	9
1762	9	nil	3	1796	9	1	3
1763	7	3	7	1797	15	2	7
1764	8	3	10	1798	10	2	8
1765	8	5	9	1799	10	2	8
1766	10	5	7	1800	11	3	5
1767	9	3	3	1801	8	5	11
1768	12	2	4	1802	16	6	5
1769	12	6	10	1803	12	2	9
1770	12	4	7	1804	8	4	5
1771	9	1	7	1805	16	4	6
1772	13	4	3	1806	9	4	28†
1773	8	2	16	1807	9	3	10
1774	17	2	3	1808	10	1	15
1775	13	1	3	1809	10	5	8
1776	14	2	2	1810	14	3	2
1777	17	1	5	1811	8	3	6
1778	9	1	8	1812	16	2	1
1779	17	4	17				

† Includes William Brice, a private of the Royal Wagon Train, drowned in the Canal, near the church.

* 9 month year, change of calendar.

Appendix V

THE 1841 CENSUS AT APPLEDORE

This gives a rather better picture of the village than the 1851 census.

There were 110 inhabited houses and 5 classified as uninhabited. Uninhabitable was probably the more accurate description. One of them housed poor Solomon Giles (see page 63). Only one of his family, his 15-year-old son, was now living with him. Also in the house were two women described as female servants. Solomon Giles, now 60, entered himself as a fishmonger.

There were 279 males and 282 females in the parish (5 of the total of 561 were sleeping rough).

The occupations of all the adults are recorded. At the top of the social scale came 14 graziers and 7 farmers. Seventeen persons are described as independent. One of these was old bankrupt George Munk aged 70 lodging with Thomas Avery, described as an agricultural labourer. Other of the independents were probably better described as old people without occupation. Next in the social scale came the surgeon, the schoolmaster and two publicans. There were many tradesmen, some just scratching a living, others comparatively well off.

Miller	(1)		Bricklayer	(1)
Shoemakers	(7)	a very high number	Glazier	(1)
			Blacksmith	(1)
Cordwainer	(1)		Dressmakers	(3)
Tailors	(2)		Fruiterer	(1)
Barber	(1)		Tea Dealer	(1)
Grocers	(2)		Butcher	(1)
Bakers	(2)		Sawyer	(1)
Fishmonger	(1)		Carpenters	(4)
Beerseller	(1)		Stackmaker	(1)
Saddler	(1)		Wheelwright	(1)

This makes 35 tradesmen, a very large number in such a small community. Another large category is that of servants, 29 females and 3 males. They worked, presumably in the graziers' and farmers' houses and for the richer tradesmen.

But far the largest section of the parish was the 60 agricultural labourers. With their usually large families they made up 238 of the total population of 561.

Appendix VI

Letter written by the Rev. William Jackson, Curate of Appledore, 1779 - 1782.

Mr. George Garnet
Greenhead
Near Kendal, Westmoreland.

Dear Cousin,

When I was last at Greenhead, just before I took my leave of the North, I promised you a line from Kent. I have deferred writing so long, that I now scarce know how to set about a business that I ought to have dispatch'd long ago.— Pardon my negligence.—
I have pleasure to inform you that I am situated in a pleasant part of the country, a part abounding with plenty of everything necessary to render living comfortable. People here are very wealthy, & live on the fat of the land. You have, doubtless, heard, or read of Romney Marsh. I am situated on the border of this marsh, about eight miles from the sea. From the church-yard I have a fine prospect of ye sea, & frequently see the ships passing to & from London. I cannot boast any thing of the healthiness of my situation; but , thank God, I have had my health very well ever since I came - never better. In the marsh there are continual fogs, morning & evening, which have a very nauseous smell, especially in the Spring & Autumn, & are reckoned very unhealthy. The marsh is all grazing land, &, for sheep the richest pasture in England. The whole marsh runs from Rye in Sussex (about eight miles from hence) to Dover, that is, above thirty miles, contains 50,000 acres, & they allow six sheep to an acre, besides the great number of bullocks that are continually grazing there.
The disorder, that is most prevalent here, is the ague, which generally, when it has once taken possession, keeps its hold for some time. I have been so lucky, so far, as to escape having one, & now, being inured to the place, am under no apprehensions of catching one. Appledore lies 64 miles south-east of London. All the country above us is intermixt with woods. The soil is very fertile, of a clayey nature, & free from stones. The by-roads are scarce passable but in summer, but the turnpike roads are in general very good. There are several places, not far from hence, that I should not chuse to live at on any acct. I cannot boast of Appledore's being a clean place, but we have this advantage, we can get out of it with ease & pleasure, on horseback in winter, into any of the great roads, which cannot be done from many places with the least degree of pleasure. The roads from Appledore are tolerable good. Appledore was once a very

91

capital town, but time, which brings everything to decay, has exerted its power here & reduced it to a very small place. Its market is gone, & it now remains only a small village. The inhabitants, my parishioners, behave to me with the greatest civility, friendship, & respect, which makes my situation very agreeable, much more agreeable than it would otherwise be. My manner of living is such as is not known in the north, but common here, & much preferable to any other mode of living. At my first coming here I gladly would have boarded, but found the people not much inclined to take in boarders, so I was obliged to have recourse to the mode of living much practiced here, & not only here but all thro' Kent & Sussex. It is customary for the Rectors, or Vicars, to allow the curates a few rooms in the parsonage house. I have two rooms, a parlour and a bed-chamber, a pantry & part of the garden, allowed to me, which are great conveniences. I give the people of the house 2s. a week, for dressing my victuals, washing, & waiting on me, which I think very reasonable. I now can have a friend, or two, to dine, or drink tea with me, at any time, without being any inconvenience or incumbrance. I frequently have some young ladies to drink tea with me; & I assure you I never lived so happy as I have done since I came here . I am frequently invited out to dine, or to tea & spend the evening, twice or thrice in a week.

I should be glad of a line from Greenhead when you can spare a little time from the more important concerns of life. I hope my uncle still continues in health. Let me be kindly remembered to him, & to Coz. Billy & his wife; and be pleased to accept of my sincerest good wishes to Mrs. Garnet & yourself.

From your ever affectionate cousin & very hble serv^t.

Wm. Jackson.

The Rev. Mr. Jackson
at Appledore
near Tenterden
Kent.

Appendix VII

APPLEDORE CHURCH

Alterations to the Fabric & Furniture 1699 - 1925

Much work was done, for better or for worse, by those responsible in the 18th and 19th centuries, for the fabric and furniture of the church. This appendix sets out what they did. It draws extensively on the records of Dr. Cock - a most reliable source. He could draw on the recollections of his grandfather who came to farm Court Lodge in 1828 and of his father. He was also at great pains to question, and record the statements of, the older inhabitants, especially Edward Avery, James Palmer and Thomas Chennell. They could remember what the church looked like before the first drastic restoration in 1858. They had heard and could remember what they were told of what happened well before then. Finally in the course of all the work which he initiated and paid for between 1909 - 1925, Dr. Cock acquired an extensive knowledge of the structure of the building.

The first alteration took place in 1699. The two big and drastic restorations in 1858 and 1888. Other work was done including Dr. Cock's own important restoration in 1924.

1699

The evidence for the 1699 work comes from a short statement which survives only because it was copied out from the old Register which ended in that year, which has long been lost. There is reason to think that the old Register was kept in one of the pubs for the convenience of parishioners, not the best way to preserve an historic record. The statement records that in 1699 'the vestry was repaired and other remarkable things done to the church both for its use and ornament by Philip Bushell, churchwarden, at the request of the vicar, John Johnston.'

Dr. Cock commenting on this statement, in the light of his knowledge of what eye witnesses told him the church looked liked before 1855, states authoritatively that the repair of the vestry in 1699 involved putting in a lathe and plaster partition to turn the North Chapel into a completely walled off room. The main wall stretched across the arch of the chancel, where the organ now is, to meet the screen which suffered the indignity of a lathe and plaster superstructure to complete the enclosure. Inside the enclosed area was another partition which divided it into two rooms. That nearest the screen was used as the village school, entered by the present vestry door (which was made at this time by

93

knocking a hole through the wall). The old sanctus bell, now hung in the Tower and known as the Tinkler, was at this time hung over this room and used as the school bell to summon the children to school. In the partition next to the nave a small window three feet high was inserted to provide a little more light. The other room was the vestry and the clergy entered the chancel through the little Tudor door which is still in use.

Dr. Cock also thinks it likely that it was at this time that the north door of the church became redundant as a result of the new door in the schoolroom, that it was filled in and its porch (of which the footings were discovered in 1925) was taken down.

What other remarkable things were done to the church by Philip Bushell we are never likely to know. However, when the plaster in the south aisle was limewashed recently, here was revealed part of a contemporary notice painted on the wall commemorating the work done by the churchwardens in 1699. Fragments of ornamentation were also found, the work either of Philip Bushell or of his much earlier predecessors.

1858.

We know a great deal about what the church looked like when Mr. Kirby was appointed vicar in 1856, before he started his restoration. He was a man of great zeal and energy. It was thanks to his initiative that the remains of the chapel of St. Mary, Ebony, on the top of the island on the site now called Chapel Bank, were taken down stone by stone, removed by horse and cart and re-erected where it now stands at Reading Street. With the same zest, he was to set out to make Appledore church fitter by the standards of mid-Victorian England to serve as a place of worship. In the process he was to destroy much that was of great interest and beauty.

When he was appointed, the church was suffering from the neglect of a century of absentee vicars. It was still a place of great beauty.

The chancel was shut off completely from the North Chapel by the school room wall. On the south side the arch between the Horne Chapel and the chancel was open and free of any clutter of choir stalls. The mullions and tracery of the east window in the chancel were almost certainly as they were in medieval times, except that the glass was plain. There had been medieval stained glass which had been taken away or lost in 1704. We know this from a note copied into the 1700 Register, which also records that this depicted ' a person in a religious habit on his knees; out of his mouth comes a labell whereof the inscription read " Newnam (?= animam) miserere Johannis Prideaux Dovorensis

94

alig^c (=? aliquando) Prioris " and underneath " Prior. Dovoricae Benefactum." " Have mercy on the soul of John Prideaux sometime Prior of Dover" and " the gift of Dover Priory". The chancel was the responsibility of the patron and up to its dissolution in 1535 the Priory of Dover had been patron of Appledore. The stonework of the east window in 1856 was, as it had been since the window was originally built.

An outside view of the church in 1809 and a sketch by R. S. Miles dated 1845 in the British Museum collection both show the framework of the arch and sill of the east window as now. The latter (reproduced in Plate 11) gives more detail of the tracery. It shows in the bottom half of the window three arched lights separated by two mullions. Above the arches are a line of five lancet openings surmounted by a single lancet This tracery would have been seen from within the chancel surrounded by the hood mould, with a man's head at each of its two bases. Dr. Cock states in many places that this hood mould is original. There is no reason to doubt this. Under the east window was the Charles II communion table, now in the Horne Chapel, and the altar rails, which have been moved from time to time to different positions in the church.

Other features in the chancel (see Plate 6) were two tie beams, one supported by a stone corbel at either end, the other by a corbel on one side, and wooden struts on the other. The Royal Arms now on the west wall then hung over the rood beam.

The Horne Chapel had no furniture and was in some decay. In particular the mullions of the south window were of wood, the stone framework having crumbled at some stage probably in the 18th century.

In the nave, the tiled floor was badly damaged in places and much of it was covered by six large box pews, some of them holding twenty or thirty persons. There was a three decker pulpit of oak and at the west end a gallery (supported on wooden pillars) which held the choir and the orchestra which had as many as eleven instrumentalists. The font was in its original position against the last pillar of the arcade, mortared to its western side.

Mr. Kirby sent out a circular appeal in 1858 for funds to finance a series of works in the church. The circular makes it clear that his main object was to put in new pews and to convert the gallery into seating for children. The children were by then taught in the new school which is still in use on the heath, but needed places in church on Sundays.

He duly carried out his plan. The old box pews were removed and replaced with modern style pews which appear in all photographs of the interior of the church up to 1925. They were then found to be worm eaten and were replaced by the oak pews now there. Before Mr. Kirby's pews could be installed he had the floor levelled and retiled on a mortar base using some of the old tiles. In the process, however, the mortar set tiles covered from view the leger stones which up to then had been part of the church floor. He also converted the gallery into a flight of benches against the west wall as seating for the children.

His zeal did not stop there. He took out the three decker pulpit and replaced it with a large new pulpit (which was in turn replaced in 1888 by the present pulpit) and hung the Royal Arms on the screen behind it. He also put in a reading desk where the lectern, presented in 1872, now stands.

At the same time, since the school room was no longer needed, he removed the whole of the partition between the chancel and the north chapel. This, as the 1870 photograph shows, was a great improvement. There was no organ nor any furniture, thus leaving a clear view of the arches opening between both chapels and the chancel. In the chancel, the only other change made by Mr. Kirby was to replace the medieval tracery in the east window with new masonry; the design followed the old pattern up to the arches of the three main lights but with the present less effective design in the top lights.

All Mr. Kirby's work shows up in the 1870 photograph. It also shows that the church was lit by candles in plain but graceful candelabra. Unfortunately it does not show the tiers of benches for the children at the west end. Another part of the restoration was the removal of the wooden circular stairway in the tower leading to the clock room. This was described by Dr. Cock's informants as a fine specimen of mediaeval carpentry. Finally Mr. Kirby planted the row of limes leading from the church yard gate to what was then the Vicarage.

1872

In this year Dr. Frederick Cock (Dr. Cock's father) had the wooden framework of the window in the south wall of the Horne Chapel replaced with the stone mullions and tracery still there. The work was done by Albert Smith for some £20. The glass was plain - replaced by G. W. Humphry's stained glass in 1925.

1888/9

Only 30 years after Mr. Kirby's restoration, as a result mainly of action by the new vicar, Mr. E. B. Russell, further drastic work was done at a cost of £800. Most of the new work was in the chancel. The two ancient tie beams were taken down, the surviving corbels, one on each side of the arcade, being left to puzzle future generations wondering what their purpose was. They, and the position they occupied, show up clearly in a photograph dated by Dr. Cock as taken in 1870 (Plate 13). The roof of the chancel was completely replaced and angle pieces, pierced with quatrefoils, designed by Mr. Day, the previous diocesan architect, were introduced to support it. Other angle pieces were put in the nave. The present clergy desks, choir stall and parclose screen were put in. All the oak timber, including that in the roof of the chancel, was handsawn in the Woodchurch yard of Mr. W. J. Bourne, who made no charge for the material or labour. The architect reponsible for the design of the furniture was Mr. Christian Evans, then diocesan architect, whose other work in Appledore is the present Court Lodge from which his standards may be judged. On the east wall round the hood mould was painted a text " I have loved thee with an everlasting love". It was still there in 1922 as a postcard shows. Later in the 30's it and similar texts elsewhere in the church were painted over. Mr. Russell's work was less drastic than Mr. Kirby's. It certainly did nothing to enhance the beauty of the church and it was not justified by the need to replace what was in disrepair.

A wooden floor was laid in the Horne Chapel, the present pulpit displaced Mr. Kirby's, the tier of benches at the west end was removed and the font shifted to its present position in the space left vacant in the south west corner. The Royal Arms were moved for the second time to their present place on the west wall. The candelabra were replaced by oil lamps, the upper half of which now enclosing electric lights are still in place.

1898 - 1900

These years saw the introduction of the Good Shepherd glass in the east window of the chancel, the design being made to fit the Kirby tracery. In 1900 the bells were taken down, most of them recast and rehung in a new frame. (see Appendix VIII.)

1909

In this year Dr. Cock repaired the outside masonry of the south window of the Horne Chapel. The inside stonework had been the contribution of his father in 1872. He also had the outside of the tower repaired down to the second string course and removed the brick filling in the 14th century windows in the north and west faces of the tower. The mullions of these windows were restored and buffer boards inserted. Dr. Cock notes that in the original medieval design the quatrefoils had been in pairs on the north, west and south sides. When the 14th-century windows were put in, the two displaced quatrefoils were replaced, one on a vacant space in the east side, the other higher up on the west. This account for the rather asymmetrical look of this part of the design.

Later work by Dr. Cock included the weather vane and its post (cost £10), the altar and sanctuary ornaments (£30) and a new paten (£7 10s.).

1924-5

In these years Dr. Cock carried out important works. The new pews put in the nave in 1858 were worm eaten and had to be thrown out. That left the pavement laid down in that year open to inspection. Dr. Cock had it all taken up (see plate 12). He recovered as many as could be saved of the 14th-century yellow and black glazed tiles 4 ins. square. These are reset on the north-west end of the nave. Some encaustic tiles of the same period and dimensions emerged which are now laid in the north-east corner of the Horne Chapel. A number of other early tiles (6 ins. x 9 ins.) of the 15th, 16th and 17th century were found and relaid. Another find under the 1858 floor was a number of leger stones with matrices in which brasses had originally been fixed. These were relaid where they could be seen in the south aisle and the centre line of the nave. Where tiles were lacking, wood blocks were laid down. On this new floor the present oak pews were placed.

Other archaeological evidence discovered was a mass of embers below the nave floor, proof of the burning of the church, almost certainly by the French in 1380. See note at the end of this appendix.

Dr. Cock's other effort was to restore and furnish the Horne Chapel. In the south window his friend G. W. Humphry designed and made the stained glass which has recently been reset to make good the distortion caused by a German bomb. In the east window Dr. Cock had the surviving medieval glass, some of it discovered when excavating the floor, reset in the top lights. Under them were placed two ancient heraldic roundels, which he had bought in Ashford. They depict the same arms (it is known from the note in the 1700 Register) as were originally in one of the windows in the Chapel— Scott impaling Lewknor and Peckham impaling Culpepper. The roundels bought by Dr. Cock are not necessarily those originally in the Chapel. Mr. Humphry designed and inserted in the same window the two pastiches. One is of the Virgin and Child in green glass (designed on the same lines as the lovely ancient glass in a window now in Stowting Church). The other depicts the last rites. Dr. Cock had new altar rails made, modelled on those originally in Newenden Church and indeed incorporating one of the original pillars of it. He repaved the floor with tiles and in the north-east corner laid the encaustic medieval tiles (unearthed when the floor of the south aisle was repaired) and in the south-east corner set the remains of the stone altar thrown out at the reformation. He repaired the altar tomb under the south window, noting that the Bethersden marble top (depicted by Muriel in a sketch in A.C. Vol. XIV) had so decayed that he had to provide a new slab made mainly of cement. He provided the new oak furniture and set up against the west foot of the arch the leger stone of Samuel Croswell who died in 1701.

In excavating the floor of the chapel he had found a brick vault with coffins of the Munk family and a few bones displaced when this was put in. He assumed that these were the bones of Philip Chute buried, according to the Bishop's Transcript of the Registers, in 1567. He could not find the leger stone which Philip Chute in his will had directed should be placed over his body, which he had also directed should be buried in the chapel. He reinterred the bones under the altar with a new stone recording his death, erroneously, in 1568.

Finally on the screen facing the congregation he had set a number of shields with the arms of two sovereigns—of Richard II in whose reign the church was burned and restored and of George V who was reigning when Dr. Cock carried out his restoration. There are also shields with the arms of the old patrons, the Priory of Dover, and of two archbishops—of Stephen Langton in whose episcopate the church was built and of Archbishop Davidson, archbishop at the time of the 1925 restoration.

Dr. Cock had done much for the church and should be remembered with gratitude.

Note on the evidence for a north aisle

There is convincing evidence that the nave originally had a north aisle with an arcade of pillars balancing those which now form the south aisle. We know that Appledore was burned by French raiders in 1380 and the 1925 excavations in the nave produced evidence in the form of masses of cinders to show that the church had been burnt. There is abundant evidence that the roof of the nave was rebuilt at about this time with a ridge and supporting crown posts out of line with the central aisle to the High Altar. This roof plan makes little sense except in the context of a decision by those who restored the church after the 1380 fire to put up a higher roof to span the area of an earlier north aisle as well as the nave. On architectural evidence therefore the theory is well supported. Dr. Cock was originally in no doubt about this. In January 1898 he wrote confidently in the Parish Magazine "There is distinct evidence, hardly comprehensible here without the help of plans and pictures, which points to the fact that the pillars and arches on the north side of the nave perished about the end of the fourteenth century and when this is taken in connection with the fact that the village was attacked and burned by the French in 1380, we may fairly conclude that some important changes took place in the interior of the church as a result of this calamity." In 1920 in his church guide he says categorically "There was formerly a north as well as a south arcade". In 1925, however, in the 5th issue of the guide he is more cautious. "There was, possibly, a north as well as a south arcade".

There is no record of how Dr. Cock's doubts arose. One relevant piece of evidence comes in a letter written to Dr. Cock on May 8th 1924 by his friend Mr. G. W. Humphry and preserved by Dr. Cock in his papers without, uncharacteristically, his usual pencilled comments. This letter brings out two facts—

    a) Dr. Cock was abroad when this part of the nave was excavated,
    b) Mr. Humphry, in his absence, watched the work and reported,
        inter alia that three stones 'were uncovered. We came across the

tops of the two lower ones (i.e. those nearest the west end) when we dug. The one nearest the chancel is much smaller. I understand that Bourne (the builder) made a note of their position for you. They were not in line but very much as I have shown them'. Unfortunately Mr. Humphry's sketch is very crude. The two bigger stones are shown as hexagonal, the smaller stone as quadrilateral.

* It and the next stone are in line with the chancel arch on the north side of the chancel. The one nearest the west door is out of line and nearer the north wall of the nave. It is relevant that in the 1938 Church Guide, written by Dr. Cock and the late G. W. Humphry, there is a "Historical Ground Plan" by Mr Elliston Erwood, the Architect, which shows the "line of a destroyed arcade" i.e. the north arcade, continuing the line of the north wall of the chancel with "foundations found 1924" marked on the line of the arcade, roughly opposite the second pillar of the south arcade.

My conjecture is that Dr. Cock's doubts arose because he was not there to inspect the evidence of the stones discovered in the excavations and felt unable to rely on the somewhat crude notes made by Mr. Humphry. It was, of course, most unfortunate that professional archaeologists were not called in to examine and record what emerged in the excavations. I think Mr. Erwood was right to conclude that what was found supported the architecturally highly probable hypothesis of a north arcade. It was unreasonable to expect to find the remnants of the footings and bases of three pillars all in line with the chancel arcade. When the damaged arcade had to be removed soon after 1380, the floor had to be levelled and any remains of the footings of the arcade had to be cut out down to the surface of the new floor or buried below it. Most of the worked stone would have been removed as valuable building material. Indeed a worked stone found in the lower wall of Mr. Moseley's home (at the back of the Bakery opposite the west door of the church) could have been part of the base of a pillar. Not much would have been left in situ.

I feel little doubt that there was a north arcade up to 1380 and that what was unearthed in 1924 supports this supposition.

* The pillars of the south arcade are octagonal. As the photographs of the excavated south aisle show, the footings are quadrilateral and only the footings of the north arcade would have survived under the pavement.

Appendix VIII

THE BELLS OF APPLEDORE

The bells and their ringers have for long been one of the glories of the church. Below is a description of them by Mr. David L. Cawley, F.S.A. Scot. who played a prominent part in the repair of the bells in 1969.

The Church Bells by David L. Cawley, F.S.A. Scot.

There are ten bells in the tower of the church, a "ring" of eight, a bell for the clock, and a small Sanctus bell.

The tower has probably always contained at least one bell to call the people to worship. As the number and power of the bells increased, so more openings were inserted in the walls to allow the sound to escape, and this may be clearly seen by the observer of the belfry windows.

Up until 1900 there were six bells and the Sanctus bell. Of these, five had been cast by the great London founder, John Hodson, whose family also had a subsidiary foundry at St. Mary Cray. The largest, or tenor, bell was cast at Ulcombe near Maidstone by the celebrated local founder Joseph Hatch. Over a hundred of his bells, cast between 1603 and 1639, still ring from Kentish steeples. The third bell was the oldest. Dating from the mid-15th century, it is originally thought that it was cast by Henry Jordan, but modern historical research indicates that it, and many like it, were probably cast around 1435 by one William Chamberlain of London. The Sanctus bell, which has no inscription, was likewise originally thought to be the old Ave bell, but a careful examination of its dimensions and mouldings during recent repairs indicated that it was probably cast in the 17th century, possibly in 1685 when four other bells were cast.

In 1900 two of the bells were found to be cracked, and a third, the tenor, had become badly broken, it is said through three drunken men making a wager that they could swing the bell upside down in three pulls one Christmas Eve! Accordingly it was decided to recast the entire peal, but in view of the antiquity of the third bell and the traditional use of the Sanctus bell (which, until 1830, hung on a frame in the North Chapel—the rope hole may be seen there— to serve as a school bell), and the efforts of the incumbent, Clifford Berney Hall, these two bells were retained. The other five were melted down, and from them the ring of eight bells at present in use was cast, by Messrs. John Warner & Sons Ltd. of London. In 1969 they and their two companions were overhauled and rehung by the

Whitechapel Bell Foundry Ltd., which has cast bells for over four hundred years.

The following are the inscriptions of the bells:

Old Peal

Treble	Iohn Hodson Mad Me 1685 I O H R Chvrch Wardns Francis Drayton Vicar.
2nd	Iohn Hodson Made me 1685 I O H R Chvrch Wardns.
3rd	Sancte Nicola Ora Pro Nbis + + + (St Nicholas Pray for Us).
4th	Iohn Hodson Made Mee 1685 Iohn Owen Henry Richardson Chrvch Wardns.
5th	Iohn Hodson Made Mee 1685 Iohn Owen Henry Richardson Chrvch W.
Tenor	Iosephvs Hatch Me Fecit 1620.

Present Bells

On all   Cast By John Warner & Sons Ltd London 1900.
Additionally, on 7th: Thomas Chennell, Giver of £100
                                Mrs. Thomas Boon £50
Additionally on Tenor: To the Glory of God.

These bells were recast and made a peal of eight in August 1900
Clifford Berney Hall, M.A. - - Vicar

Clifford Berney Hall, M.A. - - Vicar   J. C. Wright }
                                        E. B. Terry } Churchwardens

Clock Bell is the old no. 3, above.
Sanctus bell is not inscribed.

Dimensions of old and present rings

No.	Note	Diameter ins.	Weight Cwt app.
		Old	
Treble	D	31	5¼
Second	C	32	6
Third	B♭	34½	7
Fourth	A	37½	9
Fifth	G	40	11
Tenor	F	45½	15½

No.	Note	Diameter ins.	Cwt.	Qr.	Lbs.
		New			
Treble	G	27½	5	0	0
2nd	F#	28	5	1	6
3rd	E	30	5	3	17
4th	D	31½	6	0	25
5th	C	33	6	2	14
6th	B	35	7	2	25
7th	A	38	9	2	16
Tenor	G	42	12	0	15
Clock Bell	B	34½	7 approx		
Sanctus Bell		16³/₈	1 approx		

These bells are in use for the main Sunday services and also on practice nights and special occasions. For the last few minutes before the service "Tinkler" rings out (the Sanctus). Every hour of the day is marked in its passing by the beautiful clear tone of the St. Nicholas bell as sweetly as when it first came to our church five centuries ago.

INDEX

Fiennes, James, Lord Saye and Sele, 21
Fitz Wazo, 10
Forstal rebuilt (1840), 64
Fremoult, Philadelphia, 47
French raids, 15
Frencham, 40

Gavelkind, 12
George Inn, 48
Giles Solomon, pauper, 63, 75
Goldstone, Prior Thomas, 30
Goold, Rev. F., 70
Green, Henry, 61
Griffin Farm, 44
Gunter, Joan, 35

Hadrian (Emperor), 4
Haesten the Dane, 5
Haffenden, John, 46
Harman, Mary (school teacher), 71
Hastings, Battle of, 84, 85
Heath, The: 44; enclosed, 74, 76
Heath Cottage, 75
Henry VI, 20, 21
Hopton, Rev. John, 40
Horne family of Hornes Place, 14, 17, 27, 30, 31
Hornes Place: raided, 16, 17; deserted, 29
Hornes Place Chapel (licensed 1366), 15
Hulse family, 46, 66
Hulse, Gen. Sir Samuel, 65

Jackson, Rev. William, 47, 91
Jarvis, John, schoolmaster (1869-1904), 72
Jeffery, Edward, 47
Johnson, John, Vicar, 45
Johnston, Miss D., 56

Kingsnorth, Jacob, 63, 66, 72
Kings Weir, 31
Kitchyng, Rev. John, 35
Knelle family, 25, 32
Knock, 7
Knollys, Sir Henry, 17

Labourers' Revolt (1830), 62
Labourers' Wages, 58
Lanfranc, 10
Langton, Stephen, 11
Limen, river of, 1
Lollardry, 20
Long House, now the Bakery, 43
Lydd, 2, 24
Lympne, 2
Lyster, William, 40

Manor of Appledore: acquired by Canterbury Priory, 10; taken over by Dean and Chapter, 27; taken over by Ecclesiastical Commissioners, 66; rents paid to Hulses by tenants, 46; collectors' returns 1646 and 1768, 33
Market: in Appledore, 14, 74; Bailiff, 74
Market House, 43
Marsh fever, 43, 51, 57, 72
Marshall, Rev. William, 24, 51
Martello Towers, 54
Marynes, Thomas de, 37
Mass Book destroyed, 35
Mayne, Sir Anthony, 32
Medical Service for parish poor, 62
Mills and Millers, 36, 48, 49, 69
Millhouse, 40
Milton Royal, 5
Mithras Altar at Stone, 4, 78
Moyle, John, 32
Munk family, 28, 64, 65, 66

Napoleon, 53
National Trust property in Appledore, 56
Nennius, 1

Onewynne, John, 17

Paine, Thomas (Gentleman), 64
Paine, John Macket, 75
Palmer, Matthew, bricklayer, 47
Parish Council established, 73
Park Farm, 66
Parmenter, Captain, 21, 79
Paupers, 59-62
Peasants' Revolt (1381), 16
Pearson family, farmers, 66
Philip of Apoldre, 17
Pitt, William, 54
Players performances, 24
Poile, Mrs., School Governor, 72
Poor Rate, 73
Poor Relief, 59-62
Poor Row, 61, 72
Population, size of, 9, 46, 69, 76, 89
Portus Lemanis, 1
Pot Gally, 48
Pote, John, Bailiff of Manor, 31
Public Houses, 69

Queen Anne, 48
Queens Arms, 48
Queen Elizabeth, 31
Queen Margaret, 31

105